MW01491782

The ABC's of Praise

Lift Up Your Hands, Raise Your Praise and Get Lost in God

By Gloria P. Pruett

Lift Up Your Hands

Trilogy Christian Publishers

A Wholly Owned Subsidiary of Trinity Broadcasting Network

2442 Michelle Drive

Tustin, CA 92780

Copyright © 2022 by **Gloria Pruett**

Scripture quotations marked (AMP) are taken from the Amplified® Bible, Copyright © 2015 by The Lockman Foundation Used by permission.

Scripture quotations marked (CEV) taken from Contemporary English Version Copyright © 1995 American Bible Society. All rights reserved.

Scripture quotations marked (ESV) are taken from the ESV® Bible (The Holy Bible, English Standard Version®), copyright © 2001 by Crossway Bibles, a publishing ministry of Good News Publishers. Used by permission. All rights reserved.

Scripture quotations marked (NKJV) taken from the New King James Version®. Copyright © 1982 by Thomas Nelson. Used by permission. All rights reserved.

Scripture quotations marked (KJV) taken from *The Holy Bible, King James Version*. Cambridge Edition: 1769.

For information, address Trilogy Christian Publishing

Rights Department, 2442 Michelle Drive, Tustin, CA 92780.

Trilogy Christian Publishing/ TBN and colophon are trademarks of Trinity Broadcasting Network.

For information about special discounts for bulk purchases, please contact Trilogy Christian Publishing.

Manufactured in the United States of America

Trilogy Disclaimer: The views and content expressed in this book are those of the author and may not necessarily reflect the views and doctrine of Trilogy Christian Publishing or the Trinity Broadcasting Network.

10 9 8 7 6 5 4 3 2 1

Library of Congress Cataloging-in-Publication Data is available.

ISBN 978-1-68556-392-9
ISBN 978-1-68556-393-6 (ebook)

Acknowledgments

First and foremost, I'd like to thank the Movers and Shakers in my life who constantly encourage me to do what I think I can't: God my Father, Jesus my Savior and Friend and Holy Spirit my Helper and Comforter (the Man). These Three saw something in me that I never saw in myself. They encouraged me to do what I thought I couldn't. Let me also give honor to whom honor is due. Most of what you'll read came straight from Holy Spirit -- I am not that smart to come up with this. . .I'm so glad to have You Three in my life.

I want to thank my children, Charles, III (Crystal), Carlton, Sr. (Tosha), and Kelli, for loving me unconditionally, for making me laugh at mistakes, and for godly counsel. My children encouraged me to write when I did not feel like writing. Some people think they can't learn from their children. That's a lie! I can testify that you can learn from them. When it's all said and done, my children helped me be a better mommy and person. And for that, I'm truly grateful.

Finally, I want to thank the Trilogy Christian Publishing Family; my project managers (Cammy Cary), writers, proofreaders, and artists who helped me take this book to another level of Praise. I also want to thank two special friends, Dr. Stacey Hanks, and Daphne Adams for being the eyes I needed to catch errors we could not!

Table of Contents

Introduction: Don't Be Like the Nine *NEW* 1

Understanding The Concepts Of The ABC's Of Praise *NEW* 5

Allow Yourself To Experience Praise 11

Thank God For His Written Word – The Bible *NEW* 17

Bless The Lord 25

Converse With Him 31

Dare To Know All About God 35

Elevate Your Praise 41

The Father Is Waiting Just For You 53

Go For It! 59

Strictly From The Heart 63

Praising From The Valley 69

Jehovah Jireh—Our Provider 75

Keep Praising—You Have His Ear 79

Let Nothing Block You From Loving God 83

Praise When You're Naughty 93

Others In The Bible Who Praised 99

The Book Of Praise: Psalms 105

Don't Quit — Keep Praising! 111

Use Scripture As Your *ABC's Of Praise* *117*

Praise Filled With Thanksgiving 123

Potpourri Praise 127

Praise God For Courage 133

Praise God For Your Future 139

Don't Allow One Day To Spoil Your Remaining Years 145

Praise God For The United States Of America 153

I'm Free And I Love It! 159

The Earth Belongs To God, But We Get To Enjoy It! 165

Praise For Inventions 171

When The Enemy Goes Low--You Go High! *NEW* 177

A Letter Of Recommendation 183

This Chapter Is Extra Special! 187

Closing Words 191

You Pen The End 193

Alphabets I Didn't Use In A Praise *NEW* 195

INTRODUCTION

Don't Be Like The Nine!

And one of them, when he saw that he was healed, turned back, and with a loud voice glorified God,[16] *And fell down on his face at his feet, giving him thanks: and he was a Samaritan.*

Luke 17:15-16

Does God Require Praise? To answer that question, let's look at the story of the ten Lepers. If you wondered if God expects praise, this story will answer that question for you.

I confess that I was like the nine for years. While I prayed, I rarely praised. So don't think I'm throwing stones. However, once my behavior changed and I read God's word on what He expects from us, I vowed to never go back to being the ungrateful person that I once was. Let's unpack the above Scripture a little more.

Here we have ten men who had been separated from their families. They lost their jobs. These men were ostracized from society. Think about it -- a life sentence where you can no longer see your kids or family. People today have a hard time being quarantined from Covid for fourteen days, let alone a life sentence that states you can have no contact with the outside world. But one day, Jesus comes along. Let's look at the text in the Amplified. . .Luke 17:11-19 . . .*¹¹While Jesus was on the way to Jerusalem, He was passing [along the border] between Samaria and Galilee. ¹²As He entered a village, He was met by ten lepers who stood at a distance; ¹³and they raised their voices and called out, "Jesus, Master, have mercy on us!" ¹⁴When He saw them, He said to them, "Go and show yourselves to the priests." And as they went, they were [miraculously] healed and made clean. ¹⁵One of them, when he saw that he was healed, turned back, glorifying and praising and honoring God with a loud voice; ¹⁶and he lay face downward at Jesus' feet, thanking Him [over and over]. He was a Samaritan. ¹⁷Then Jesus asked, "Were not ten [of you] cleansed? Where are the [other] nine? ¹⁸Was there no one found to return and to give thanks and praise to God, except this foreigner?*

Here it is, my proof that Jesus expects praise when He does something for us. Let's continue, *¹⁹Jesus said to him, "Get up and go [on your way]. Your faith [your personal trust in Me and your confidence in God's power] has restored you to health."*

Jesus did what Jesus does, He healed all ten. What's interesting about this story is that none returned to give thanks but the one.

It boggles the mind. You can now return to your life, but can't thank the One who gave you your life back? It's something so wrong with that story. In verse 17, we see how Jesus feels. He asks the one, *"Were there not ten cleansed? But where are the nine?"*

I could really pull this apart and preach to you via this book, but I won't. However, let me ask this question. How often do we act like the nine? How often are we so happy that God came through for us that we give a praise report to all those around us but forget to praise God? Let's not do that. These men were so caught up in the fact that they were healed that they forgot about Jesus.

Jesus just gave them their life back. They could finally see their kids, reunite with their wives, start working again being a productive citizens of society once more and all they could do was walk away from the One who healed them?

How much does Jesus have to give us before we give Him praise? He gave you another job with better pay when you didn't praise Him for the first two. You're on husband number two when you didn't praise Him for husband number one. You got a new home when you didn't praise God for the beautiful rental He gave you with low rent.

When do you think He deserves praise? From this day forward, decide, if you're not doing it already, that you will be someone who praises God. Praise Him for a new day. Praise Him when you get your hair done and the clouds come, but He lets you get home before the rain begins to pour. Praise Him when you bowl 299, that He let you get that close to 300. (I know some of y'all may not agree with that one ☺.)

When you're driving past a hospital and you realize, you don't know anyone who is in a hospital; you're not and neither are any of your relatives. I think that deserves a hefty praise.

God's word is clear on praise and here is one Scripture I'll repeat over and over, Psalms 150:6 which says, *"Let everything that hath breath praise the Lord. Praise ye the Lord."*

You don't want Jesus, who sits at the right hand of the Father, to look over at Him and say, *"Didn't We just open the door for them to get a new home with their jacked-up credit? Did you hear anything Father? I didn't. Didn't We just give them their dream job? Did you hear anything Dad? And then Jesus says, let's not charge it against them. We know they will get it right."* Your grace still covers the ungrateful. WOW!

As you begin to write your praises, be on the lookout for "trigger words" that jump out at you and will take your praise higher. Words you've not used before when giving praise to God!!

For example, I was reading something about someone becoming "confused" about something. That word "confused" jumped in my spirit and right there, I praised God for helping me to not become confused by the enemy's words that would have me think that God had left me. Confused that He still loved me in spite of what I did recently. No, I'm not "confused." God loved me enough to give His only Son for me and He's not changed, He still loves me. I praise God that I'm stable in my thoughts about His love for me.

Again, I would have NEVER thought of using the word confused in praising God, but once you begin to search out words, you'll find yourself thinking outside the box when it comes to praise.

As this chapter comes to a close, let's remember the LEPERS and vow to not be like them. Tell God, "You've done so much for me, and I admit there have been times in my life that I've forgotten to praise You. If I were truly honest, I've ignored You when it was You who cleansed me. I left you hanging. I gave You no spiritual handshake. I showed no appreciation. Flat out I failed to say thank You! But this story has lit a fire under me to do better and I will." That's what God needs to hear from us and from this day forward, let's not withhold our praise! Together, let's go higher!

Understanding The Concepts Of The ABC's Of Praise

Just what ARE the ABC's of praise? I am glad you asked. The ABC's of praise is a concept that will keep you focused on God and not on your surroundings as you praise Him. It never failed that long ago, before I learned this concept, my mind would be all over the place as I tried to praise, especially when I was trying to do it at home. When you're in church it can be easier, because you have the praise leader as a cheerleader, cheering you on. But to be honest, I believe we get more kudos from God when we praise Him and no one else is around. That's my personal opinion.

The **A** represents Your **A**ctions which should convey your gratitude or gratefulness to God daily.

I'm going to give you the simplest definition of the word action. It means a thing done; an act. Actions imply movement, you do something. Your actions really tell how you feel about someone or something. If I'm unhappy with you or don't want to be around you, you'll know it by the way I respond to you, either verbally or through my body language, even if I never say a word. But when it comes to God, we need to say it!! We need to convey our gratefulness to Him.

How?

That's where the **B** comes in. You do it by **Boasting** about your Father God, **Boasting** about your Savior and Lord, Jesus, boasting about your Best Friend Holy Spirit. **Boast** about them first, then about others second.

What exactly is boasting? Not what one thinks, because we're not touting our accomplishments. We're touting with pride what God has done for us.

When you boast about someone, there is no room for doubt that they are special to you. Here though is what some of us do. We tell others how good God is. We tell them how grateful we are for blessings we receive from God. We share the wonderful things our children or siblings are doing with others. But many times, we fail to thank God or tell Him how wonderful He is.

It's like the story of the couple who went to a marriage counselor. The wife went on for fifteen minutes talking about all the things her husband does wrong and she ends with, "He hasn't told me he loves me since the day we were married!"

The minister then says, "Wait a minute. I don't believe for one second that the two of you have been married for thirty-five years, and he hasn't told you he loves you since your wedding day. That's inconceivable." He then turns to the husband and says, "Tell me she's exaggerating. You have told your wife many times since your wedding day that you love her, right?"

The husband looks at the minister with a puzzled look on his face and says, "Now she's telling the truth on that one! No. I haven't told her I love her since our wedding day. I told her then and nothing's changed, I still love her. I'll let her know when it changes!"

That may sound humorous, but we do God like that. We get saved, and for a while we're good at boasting to Him about how grateful we are, then after a while, we stop. I'm encouraging you to not stop!

By **boasting and telling** God all that He's done for you, which I'm sure is a lot, that alone will keep you praising for a while. Make sure you praise Him for your family and friends as well!

Let God know you appreciate Him by saying out loud that you love Him. You're thankful that He forgives your sins.

Thank Jesus for interceding to the Father on your behalf daily! Dying was enough, but He still intercedes for you. He gave His precious blood for us! He's the One who gave us Holy Spirit! Tell Jesus that you're honored He gave you your BFF (Best Friend Forever) in the person of Holy Spirit.

Let Holy Spirit know you're grateful that He is there to guide you in your victories as well as your failures. Say thank You, Holy Spirit, when He reminds you of where your keys are. Tell Him what a great Helper He is!

Now the important one -- **C**, which stands for **Consistency.** Don't be a yoyo Praiser. You don't want to tell God how good He is one day and not praise Him for three days. **Be consistent** with your praise.

When you praise every day, sometimes it may feel like you're being repetitive, and you could have the tendency to get bored and stop. What does being repetitive have to do with anything? We don't have an issue receiving repetitive blessings, do we?

That's one of the reasons I wrote this book; Once you understand the principle, you won't feel like you're saying the same things over and over.

Once you grab hold of the concept, you won't have that problem. But like a good novel, I won't give it away just yet. I will tell you this, I believe this book will give you "fresh ways" to express your love, and you won't get bored with your praise.

One last thing. It's so important to be thankful when someone does something for you, especially Our Heavenly Father along with Jesus, His Son, and Holy Spirit. And guess what, the circumstances around your praise may not always be good, but there is always good in it.

I Thessalonians 5:18 says we are to give thanks IN everything, not for everything. The actual Scripture reads, *¹⁸ In every thing give thanks: for this is the will of God in Christ Jesus concerning you."*

Here's an example of that Scripture. You finished shopping at the grocery store and headed for the parking lot. (This really happened to a friend of mine.) You took the groceries that were in the cart, put them in the SUV, took the cart to the cart stall, but somehow you get distracted because a couple is arguing, and you leave your purse in the cart.

You have your wallet and keys in your hand, so you don't notice you left your purse until you get to your next destination which is ten miles away.

Right there you have an opportunity to praise God that you have your keys and your wallet. That's what it means by praising God in everything.

But the story doesn't end there. You call the store and get put on hold, so you raced back to the grocery store, walk up to customer service to be greeted by the manager who before you can say anything she says to you, "Are you the lady who left your purse in the cart?" Heart racing you say, "Yes!" The manager replies, "I have it; someone turned it in. Wait here just a moment and I'll get it for you." What the manager does not know is that in your purse was $1,500 cash that you withdrew from the bank for a bill. As she hands you the purse, you can't wait to look inside to find everything in order the way you left it. The envelope containing the $1,500 was still tucked in the inside zipper compartment untouched.

Now if that's not a reason to go Hallelujah crazy, I don't know what is. But remember, we're talking about in everything give thanks.

Using this story as our example, don't forget to praise God because you didn't get a ticket for speeding back to the grocery store. You didn't get in an accident and the angels watched over your belongings! And while you're thanking Him, ask Holy Spirit to keep you focused next time so you won't leave your purse!

So, for those of you who read my first version of *Lift Up Your Hands, Raise Your Praise and Get Lost in God*, I strongly encourage you to read this version. Holy Spirit gave me so much "New" insight that I don't want you to miss any of it!

Let's recap. The ABC's stands for; **A** is for **Action**, you have to do something. **B** stands for **Boasting**, not on yourself, but on God. And **C,** again, is the most important one, be **Consistent**.

Remember, **YOU MAY NOT ALWAYS HAVE A Z WORD. DON'T WORRY ABOUT IT. Just be happy and praise!**

Now, sit back, relax, get a cup of hot chocolate or a glass of lemonade, whichever applies and enjoy the nuggets between these pages as we, together, begin our journey and delve into the concept of the *ABC's of Praise*. C'mon, let's *"Lift Up Our Hands and Raise our Praise and Get Lost In God."*

Allow Yourself To Experience Praise

Let everything that hath breath praise the Lord, Praise
ye the Lord.

Psalms 150:6

I wrote this book over fifteen years ago. Since then, I have continued to praise God and pen more praises. I thought it was time to
revise my earlier manuscript to include some of the newly revealed
things I've learned about praising God. One thing that will never
change, you will always have something new to praise God for. It
never gets old, just sweeter.

While there are several new praises, I have reworked and re-
wrote and retouched almost every praise listed.

My grandmother was a pastor and, from the time I was in my
mother's arms until now, I have always been in somebody's church
forty-five (or more) Sundays of every year. I was taught many
things: Live right, and you will please God; if you don't live right,
God will punish you. And depending on the church I attended,
God's only directive seemed to be the Do Not's – do not do this,
do not do that. But the subject of praise and how to do it never
came up. When I went to church, we sang A and B selections.

I've attended many churches in my life, but it wasn't until
1986, when I joined a church where the pastor taught the Word

of God directly from the Bible, that my life literally changed. I actually had to take a Bible to church. The pastor actually read more than three Scriptures. Suddenly, I began to see things in the Bible that I had never seen before. I began to experience things that I had never experienced before, like praising God and praying in the Holy Spirit [a.k.a. praying in tongues]. As often as I attended churches in the past, I had never felt nor was I taught these things. How sad not to be exposed to something so beautiful as praise and praying in tongues!

If my calculation is correct, I have been offering praise to God for about twenty years. Around 2004, many years later, my praise took a turn for the better and was more heartfelt. What do I mean by that? I mean the praise that came from my lips was a deep, earnest, sincere praise. Yet it saddens me that I had been a Christian for most of my life and had missed out on so much. What happened back then? Was God not good to me in my twenties? Had He done nothing in my life in my 30's? Why so many years of lost gratitude? No consistent "thank you?" No "I so appreciate you!" Yes, every now and then I was thankful. You know, you get a raise, and your hands go up with a "Thank You, Jesus!" But nothing consistent. Didn't He deserve consistent praise? Sure He did! But because I was not taught to praise, it was not on my to-do list. This is not something I'm proud of, but I share it with you because I want you to know that even if you aren't praising God now, you can start. And if you are praising Him, you can use my *ABC's of Praise* to take your praise to the next level.

I have been called to share what I've learned about praise to help you **develop** and **enhance** your praise to God. I want your personal praise time, the time you spend at home or when you're alone in the car, or walking -- just anytime you find yourself alone,

I want your praise to be so sweet and special that you get "lost" in your praise and expressions of gratitude. You won't even know what time it is; you'll be so focused on your praise.

The main emphasis of this book will be your personal, intimate time with God – praising Him. If you learn to praise when no one is watching or cheering you on at church, then the praise leader at church won't have to work as hard for you to enter in.

For those of you who aren't sure why you should praise at home besides the fact that the Bible tells us we should praise God, let's look at the following scenario:

A married couple is in a crowd. The husband is found holding his wife's hand, smiling, and gazing into her eyes and saying all the right things. He even whispers sweet somethings in her ear. The crowd sees him and approves. "He's the man," they murmur, and they secretly admire him. However, as soon as this couple gets in their car and vanishes from the eyesight of others, the husband, who was so loving in front of the crowd, suddenly shuts down. He ceases to say nice things to his wife. He rarely looks at her. He totally ignores her until they are once again in the presence of other people. You can imagine how his wife must feel! This also goes for a wife who would do what I've just described.

Well, God has feelings too! Don't you think He wonders why you praise Him in church but ignore Him when you are alone – just you and Him – together? I'm not talking about the daily "Thank You for waking me up. Thank you for my job." How about stretching your hands in the air when you wake up in the morning and saying, "Heavenly Father, You've given me so much to be grateful for, let me just honor You before I do anything else. Let me start by thanking You for giving up your Son! I would not have done it! Good morning, Jesus, my Savior. How wonderful to get up and be in the presence of such Royal Guests. Holy Spirit, my treasured Friend, once again I can do the impossible because I have You as my hanging Buddy." That beats a cup of coffee first thing any day. Let us experience daily how sweet it is to declare continued praise to our God.

After reading this book, and implementing its concepts, you won't be a clock-watcher; you'll be a thinker. If you are a drifter during praise, you'll become challenged. Time will fly and you'll have fun telling God how you feel about Him. What a great place to be!

Once you begin to use these concepts of the *ABC's of Praise*, your thoughts will quickly lineup with your desire to shut out everybody and everything. You won't have to struggle, because the concepts will make you think only about God. You will no longer be a clock watcher during prayer and praise.

When I began to focus on praise, I established various times for personal devotion. To this day, years later, I still must fight for this, because something always wants to steal the Lord's time from us. The world is vying for your time. Your babies want your time. The TV has programs designed for you. Let's not talk about the computer with YouTube, Instagram, emails, Facebook, and Twitter! Let's not forget the real culprit found in John 10:10 which says, *[10] The thief cometh not, but for to steal, and to kill, and to destroy: I am come that they might have life, and that they might have it more abundantly.* The thief here is the devil!! He wants to steal your praise!!! Don't let him!

So how did my journey begin where I made the decision to change and go higher? I just got sick and tired of rote praise. It went like this. During devotion, I reserved a portion of time for praise, prayer, reading of the Word, and writing down my thoughts, beginning with five minutes allotted for each. Eventually, I increased my time. But I discovered the praise portion always got cheated and that bothered me. I was determined to do something about it.

Lack of time spent wasn't the only issue I had during my time of praise. I said all of the "right things," "I love You, Lord." "I glorify Your Name." "I thank You for being Lord over my life." "Hallelujah, You deserve the highest praise." "I bless You, Lord." I said all the traditional stuff. I did that for years until one day I came clean before God. I flat out asked Him, "Don't You get tired of hearing me say the same things over and over?" I was tired of hearing myself. Was I expressing to God how I felt about Him at that moment? Or was I repeating what I had always said? I was in a rut!! How did I *really* feel? Was I saying what was in my heart?

I finally asked Holy Spirit, "Please teach me how to love God with my whole heart. Help me to speak beyond my current vocabulary. Help me express to God daily what He means to me. Help me to not sound like a broken record, day in and day out. God deserves so much more from me and you. I asked Holy Spirit, "Help me Holy Spirit articulate to God, and my Lord Jesus, and to You, the very fact that I would be lost without You Three."

When you cry out for help from your Helper, He will answer your prayers. When He answered me, the concept of this book was birthed.

Using the *ABC's of Praise* will get your mind and spirit to cooperate with each other for a common goal of uninterrupted, raw praise. No other outside thoughts will dominate your time (i.e., "What's for dinner? I've got to go to the cleaners! I do not believe he said that to me today!"). You will successfully keep your mind and spirit solely on God as you enter and exit your praise.

Praise is a magnificent tool! Heartfelt praise is even more satisfying. Praise is a win-win situation. God gets the glory, and you leave His presence with a Kool-Aid™ smile on your face that no devil in hell can erase. Your life may still be the same as when you began to praise, but being in God's presence is a confidence builder. Now you can see yourself healed! You can sense your victory! You know you can win in life!

Sincere praise will erase depression, and your focus will not be on your cares. You will become lighter, more confident and feel as though you can conquer the world. But it takes more than two minutes. Praise is not something you do once a day along with your devotion. You may begin that way, but you will not continue that way. Praise, like prayer, is a way of life, and once you begin to use the concepts in this book, you will come to love it. As you begin to apply the principles outlined on the pages that follow, you too will come to a place where you will get "lost in HIM."

Thank God For His Written Word – The Bible

This book of the law shall not depart out of thy mouth;
but thou shalt meditate therein day and night, that thou
mayest observe to do according to all that is written
therein: for then thou shalt make thy way prosperous,
and then thou shalt have good success.

Joshua 1:8-9

The Bible is still the bestselling book ever written, and, as Christians, we ought to read God's Word. Remember to never underestimate, nor dismiss, the written Word of God. It's His love letter to you! The Word is our spiritual compass. And, with Holy Spirit's help, the Word will guide us through life, causing us to navigate raging waters and arrive safely to our destinations and reveal God's will for our lives. God's Word is the light that illuminates our paths (Psalms 119:105).

When I checked the *Guinness World Records* on Saturday, November 6, 2021, under the heading of "Best Selling Book," guess what tops the list? It's the Bible. The numbers sold said 5,000,000,000 UNIT(S) SOLD. I can't even tell you how many that is!!

The influence on the human heart, lives that have been won to Jesus, stories that make us want to do right, are just some of the benefits of reading God's Word. We should never forget to thank God for this incredible resource that's at our fingertips!

Having technology that will assist us in reading our Bible is good. However, let me encourage you to never replace the written Word in ink on paper with your cell phones and tablets. Those resources should be added tools, not replacement tools.

About ten years ago while preaching around the United States, Holy Spirit revealed something to me. He said, "When the electricity goes out and chargers don't work, you need something tangible that you can hold and refer to! Always, always, keep your paper Bible printed in ink."

Below are thirty-one plus reasons to praise and thank God for our Bible – His written Word. It's a small list but, prayerfully, it will make you thirsty for more. If I were a betting woman, and I'm not, most of you reading this could come up with something more creative than what I've written, and I'm going to encourage you to do so. But to get you started, here is what I've penned. Before reading, just lift your hands and repeat something of this nature.

Heavenly Father, in the Name of Jesus, there is so much in Your Word to be grateful for, so as I confess to You what Your written Word means to me, just know I'm thankful for each declaration.

If not for Your Word God, I wouldn't know that I had an **Advocate** in the person of Holy Spirit, **S**omeone Who would help me fight. If not for Your Word God, I wouldn't know that I don't have to be **A**nxious in life. (Philippians 4:6-7, NKJV)

It was Your Word that told me I would be **Blessed** in life if I adhered to Your laws. But You also told me what would happen if I didn't, and it's not good. (Deuteronomy 28)

Jesus, Your Word told me if I would **Confess** my sins to You that You would be faithful and just to forgive me and cleanse me from all unrighteousness and that You would remember my sins no more. This is a huge benefit that I'm eternally grateful for. (I John 1:9 & Hebrews 8:12)

If not for Your Word, God, I wouldn't know I could be **Delivered** from the hand of the enemy. (Psalms 18:17)

If not for Your Word I wouldn't even know who my **Enemy** was; I'd think it was my boss, people in general. You even told me his name – the devil! (1 Peter 5:8-9)

If not for Your Word God, I wouldn't know how to get **Friends**. All I need do is show myself friendly. (Proverbs 18:24)

If not for Your Word God, I wouldn't know that all **Generations** (nations) would be blessed because of Abraham's obedience. All Generations include me and my kids and grandkids. Yes, we are blessed! (Genesis 22:18)

If not for Your Word, I wouldn't know I could be **Healed.** (Isaiah 53:4-5 – I Peter 2:24)

If not for Your Word God, I wouldn't know that nothing is **Impossible** with You. I can do anything! (Luke 1:37) Your Word also declares that I'm made in Your **Image**. You could have made me like one of the animals, but I'm made in Your very **Image**. (Genesis 1:26)

If not for Your Word, I wouldn't even know that **Jesus,** precious **Jesus,** didn't come to the earth to make a Name for Himself. He suffered a horrific death. Why did He come? To seek and save the lost. That was me. I'm so grateful. (Luke 19:10)

If not for Your Word God, I wouldn't know that wise men lay up **Knowledge.** (Proverbs 10:14) You warned that a lack of **Knowledge** causes people to be destroyed, and You said that You would reject me if I rejected **Knowledge.** I'm not going to let that happen. Thanks for telling me what knowledge will do." (Hosea 4:6)

If not for Your Word God, I wouldn't know how much I was **Loved.** You allowed Your only Son, Jesus to suffer and die so that I could be redeemed from hell and have everlasting life. Because of your Love for the world, Jesus came and suffered, for me -- what love. (John 3:16)

Thank You Jesus for the warning in Your Word of loving **Money.** You've told us it's the root of all evil, and some Christians have left the faith, because of their love for **Money.** You never said money was bad, You just told us to not love it! I love You Lord, not **Money.** (I Timothy 6:10)

If not for Your Word God, I wouldn't know that when I feel alone, You haven't gone anywhere. Your Word tells me if I draw **Nigh** to You that You would draw **Nigh** to me! (James 4:8)

If not for Your Word God, I wouldn't know my belief in Jesus as Your Son assures me that I can **Overcome** the world. (I John 5:5)

If not for Your Word I wouldn't know that You, the God of the Universe, had a **Plan** for my life to **Prosper** me. **Plans** to give me a hope and a future. WOW! (Jeremiah 29:11)

If not for Your Word God, I wouldn't know that one of the reasons You gave me the shield of faith was so that I could **Quench** [extinguish] the fiery darts of the enemy. (Ephesians 6:16)

If not for Your Word Lord, I wouldn't know that I could **Resist** the devil and he would **Run** (flee) from me. I stopped running from him once I found this out. (James 4:7)

If not for Your Word, I wouldn't know that I could be **Saved** (born again) and go to Heaven when I leave this earth by believing that Jesus is the Son of God and confessing with my mouth that Jesus is my Lord and Savior (Romans 10:9-10). If not for

Your Word I wouldn't know that reading The Bible assures me of **Success.** (Joshua 1:8-9)

If not for Your Word God, I wouldn't know that Holy Spirit could help me **Tame my Tongue.** I can't do it by myself but with Holy Spirit's help my tongue can be tamed. (James 3:8)

If not for Your Word God, I wouldn't have read where you warned me to not be **Unequally** yoked with **Unbelievers.** I am commanded to love them, but they should not be my hanging buddies. You have a standard, and I must adhere to it! (II Corinthians 6:14)

If not for Your Word, God, I wouldn't know that You said I don't have to avenge myself because it's written that **Vengeance** belongs to You and You said You'd repay folks who mess with me. So, I'm free; it's time for me to stop trying to repay people for what they've done, I'll just pray for them. I'll leave **Vengeance** in Your capable hands! (Romans 12:19)

If not for Your Word God, I wouldn't know that when I need **Wisdom**, I can just ask You and You will give it to me. Not just a little but You'd give it to me generously and You won't correct me for asking. (James 1:5) Your Word also assures me that any **Weapon** formed to harm me will not prosper! So, I don't have to be afraid! (Isaiah 54:17)

If not for Your Word God, I wouldn't know that I don't have to feel tired and lifeless. You said in Your Word that You satisfy me with good things and that my **Youth** is renewed as the eagle's. (Psalms 103:5)

If not for Your Word God, I wouldn't know that You expect me to be **Zealous** [passionate] for You. You don't like lukewarm, so I'll stay on fire for You and refuse to be lukewarm. **Zealous** is what I will be! Thank You Jesus for sharing Your Heart and letting me know Your expectations. (Revelations 3:19)

Thank You God for Your Written Word!

Before I close this chapter, I'd like to share with you something God gave me years ago. He told me to make this confession each time I preached, as well as each time I opened my Bible to study, even if it was just Holy Spirit and me doing some study together.

If I were to be honest, for the first three or four years I didn't even do it while preaching. My flesh told me it was corny. My flesh told me it was carnal, and I was just trying to be like other preachers who had a "confession" before they preached. So, I only did it during my personal time with the Lord. Just in case you haven't figured it out yet, partial obedience is disobedience, and I was being disobedient. Yes, I was reluctant to do all that God told me because I was afraid of people.

Well, I got free, and I began to say my confession, in the pulpit and in private. To my surprise, people began to ask me if I had it written down because they wanted to confess it as well when they were doing their personal Bible study. So, I'm going to give it to you as well and if Holy Spirit leads you, it's here for your use. . .

Lift your Bible in the air or hold it over your heart and repeat this. Father, Your Word is precious to me. And from this day forward when I think, hear, or read Your Word, I'm reminded that the **W** in Word tells me that it **W**orks. Not just sometimes but all the time. The **O** in Word says as I **Obey** Your Word, I'll **O**vercome just like You said I would. And because I'm an **O**vercomer, the **R** in Word tells me that I **Reign** in this life. And because I **Reign**, the **D** assures me that what I **Decree** shall be! So, Father, thank You for Your Word that Works! In Jesus's Name, Amen.

Once you say this confession, start to read the Word. Remember what you just confessed, believe what you just read and confessed is not only true but it's there for you, and you'll have what you decree!

STOP

Start

BLESS THE LORD

> *Bless the Lord, O my soul: and all that is within me, bless his holy name.*

Psalms 103:1

Praise can be defined in many ways. It can mean to extol in words or song, to magnify, to glorify excellent works, or to express gratitude for personal favors or benefits received.

One Bible dictionary defines praise as: "One of humanity's many responses to God's revelation of Himself. . .Praise comes from a Latin word meaning 'value' or 'price.' Thus, to give praise to God is to proclaim His merit or worth."

If you have seen any of God's excellent works or if you are grateful for anything God has done for you and you admire God, then you should praise Him. Scripture tells us that if we are breathing, we should praise (Psalms 150:6).

We all like it when someone gives us praise. Everyone enjoys compliments. Suppose you finally bought a new suit with shoes and a purse to match? Your hair and makeup are fresh. You splurged and got the ultimate female combo (I'm not talking about a burger, fries, and a drink – I'm talking about the ultimate manicure and pedicure). You would have a fit if no one gave you a compliment at least once.

Men are no different. Your suit was made especially for you, your designer socks peek below the cuffs of your pants as you sit, and your shoes has to have the "boss gloss." Your tie and hanky are screaming along with your fresh hair cut saying, "Look at me!" Tell me you don't swell when the compliments follow.

According to Genesis 1:26-27: *"And God said, Let us make man in our image, after our likeness: ...So God created man in his own image, in the image of God created he him; male and female created he them."* If we are made in the image and likeness of God and we like praise, wouldn't it stand to reason that God Himself likes praise? Sure, He does. Remember, we read earlier about the Nine?

Later as you read some of the scriptures herein, you will again be reminded that God not only likes praise, He expects it from us. God's Word in Psalms 150:6 confirms that God expects praise.

Remember this: Everything belongs to God. It all started with Him. Thus, if everything you own belongs to God – He's letting you use His stuff. It's only right to thank Him for using what's His. Psalms 24:1 says, *"The earth is the Lord's, and the fullness thereof; the world, and they that dwell therein."* This is repeated in I Corinthians 10:26, *"For the earth is the Lord's and the fullness thereof."* Let's look at the same verse from the Amplified Bible: *"For the [whole] earth is the Lord's and everything that is in it."* Exodus 19:5(b) says, *"...all the earth is mine."* Deuteronomy 10:14, *"Behold, the heaven and the heaven of heavens is the Lord's thy God, the earth also, with all that therein is."*

God owns everything! Even the air you breathe. If God decided to cut off our oxygen right now, and I'm not talking about what's in a tube that can be purchased (that's His too), none of us would be able to live. We couldn't even breathe without God! I'm going to paraphrase a joke I heard someone tell to illustrate my point.

Several scientists went to God and told Him they figured out how to make a man without His help. Their man proved to be equal to the one He made. God's reply was, *"Really?"* With a smirk on their faces and standing in a pool of arrogance— they replied, "Really!" God then told them, "Go ahead, let Me see what you can do." They began to pull their resources from a trunk, starting with a wad of dirt. God quickly interrupted—took the dirt and politely said, "Get your own dirt—this belongs to Me."

You see, everything belongs to God. It's our duty and our privilege to praise Him!

When I spend time in God's presence, I feel like I can do anything. I feel like *Somebody*, because I'm in the presence of *Somebody!* My earthly situation before praise may be the same as it is after praise, but being in God's presence affects me in a positive way. The Word of God will have that same effect on you. You will be enlightened. You will read something several times, and suddenly Holy Spirit will give you a new revelation that you never saw before. After reading His promises, you will experience hope that you never felt before.

Praise has one condition, however. If you want to feel good about what you're saying, then you need to have a personal relationship with God.

What if I said, "What a beautiful suit you had on last week," yet I didn't see you last week. You might respond by saying, "I don't own a suit, and I've never worn one." Wouldn't I feel dumb? I was trying to give you praise when I really didn't know you. If I really knew you, I would have known that you didn't own a suit. Don't continue trying to praise God because of what you heard someone else say. Get to know Him and praise Him because of what you know about Him and what you know will make you lift up your hands in praise.

God's Word tells us what He expects from us. His Word describes His character, and it tells us about Him as a Person. It tells us what He's done for us and what we can expect Him to do in the future. When you take time to read God's Word and realize what He's done for you, you're better equipped to give Him the praise He deserves. You can accurately thank Him from the bottom of your heart.

The Bible, coupled with your life history, will give you all you need to know to praise God. We all have much to praise God for—our families, the predicaments He's gotten us out of, His mercy regarding our thoughts alone. That is enough to keep our hands lifted high in praise and thanksgiving.

Let's reflect on your thoughts for a moment. God's forgiveness from our thoughts ought to cause us to extend our hands in praise. I know my thoughts and I know I'm not alone! I'm talking about vile, ugly thoughts. Clearly, God knows every thought that comes to your mind. Matthew 9:4 says, *"And Jesus knowing their thoughts said, 'Wherefore think ye evil in your hearts?'"* Matthew 12:25 reads, *"And Jesus knew their thoughts . . ."*

You cannot allow your thoughts to run wild with sin. If the enemy brings you a thought and you cast it down, you have no problem with God. However, if you take that thought and begin to meditate on it, turning it over and over in your mind, that thought now becomes *yours* and not the devil's. You've taken that small thought and composed many thoughts from it. We need to do what 2 Corinthians 10:5 says, *"Casting down imaginations, and every high thing that exalteth itself against the knowledge of God and bringing into captivity every thought to the obedience of Christ."*

When a thought comes that is not of God, our responsibility is to "cast it down," not salivate and take possession of it.

I'm not just talking about those lustful and evil things that you know come from the enemy. I'm talking about the ones you've conjured up as well. Some of us have murdered more people in our thoughts than serial killers who are locked up in prison. Some of us have gone to bed with more men and women than King Solomon, and that's a lot. And some of you have slapped your mother-in-law in your thoughts just this past week. The poor woman was holding her jaw, shocked and what you did to her.

How many times have we strangled our boss in our minds? Too many to number! I'm making this comical because it goes down a little easier, but it's true.

These thoughts alone could land you in hell, but God through His mercy and grace, forgave us and held back the penalty of our thoughts. If you can't think of any reasons to praise God, *praise Him for not putting us in hell for our thoughts!* Proverbs 23:7 clearly says, *"For as he thinketh in his heart, so is he."* Unchecked thoughts will produce—good or bad! So, watch your thoughts.

Let's lift our hands right now and say, "Thank You, Father, for having mercy on me and my thoughts. Thank You for not condemning me when I meditate on things that I know are not pleasing in Your sight. I'll honor You in my thoughts. From this day forward, I'll be careful and cast down anything in my thought life that's not pleasing to You."

You should praise God for everything, but you will have trouble praising someone you don't know. You can only go so far, and then you're stuck. For example, what if your mother bought you three dresses: one black, one blue, and one brown. You could begin to shower praises on her for being so nice, so thoughtful, so caring. You could think of many things to say to your mother to thank her for those dresses and her generosity. You might even say, "Mom, thank you for blessing me with these three dresses. You're the best mother in the world!"

But what if someone blessed you with three dresses and the gift was anonymous? Your praise would change. You could give praise for the gift, but you wouldn't know *who* to praise. This is what happens when you really don't know God. You believe the tangible things you acquire are a result of something you did. You paid your money for your clothes. You went to school, and you deserved the promotion you got. But look at Psalms 75:6–7, *"For promotion cometh neither from the east, nor from the west, nor from the south . . . But God is the judge: he putteth down one, and setteth up another."* 1 Samuel 2:7 also says something similar to this, *"The Lord maketh poor, and maketh rich: he bringeth low and lifteth up."*

If you didn't know it before, you know now from Scripture that God owns everything. He is the Boss. Surely, He deserves our praise.

Converse With Him

Enter into his gates with thanksgiving, and into his courts with praise: be thankful unto him, and bless his name.

Psalms 100:4

It's difficult to talk to someone you don't know and you can't praise someone you don't talk to. God knows you—get to know Him.

I can't take for granted that everyone reading this book understands that God wants us to talk to Him. Consider these Scriptures, 1 John 1:3, *"That which we have seen and heard declare we unto you, that ye also may have fellowship with us: and truly our fellowship is with the Father, and with his Son Jesus Christ."* 1 Chronicles 16:11 says, *"Seek the LORD and his strength, seek his face continually."* John 15:16 tells us, *"Ye have not chosen me, but I have chosen you, and ordained you, that ye should go and bring forth fruit, and that your fruit should remain: that whatsoever ye shall ask of the Father in my name, he may give it you."*

These Bible references refer to fellowship, seeking God, and asking Him for things. We need to ask God to help us develop good attitudes, godly character, integrity, patience, peace, and so forth. We don't have a problem asking for money, cars, and houses. Does God want us to have those things? Yes! He wants us to have those things. But we also need character builders so we can handle the other blessings. And we build our character by talking to God and reading His Word.

As a child and during my teens, and to be very transparent, even in my twenties, I rarely held conversations with God. I said my prayers before I ate and at night before I went to bed, but holding a conversation with Him, just to talk, rarely did I do that. That kind of talk was reserved for adults and ministers.

Think about it, if you don't talk to Him, you certainly can't praise Him like you should. I believed my grandmother talked to God for me. After all, she was a pastor, and God always talks to pastors—and other adults who were chosen by Him, but not just ordinary people— so I thought!

These childhood experiences with God remind me of a little girl I once saw at a baby shower. The adults were conversing with one another, and it was obvious, once you noticed her, that she was in a deep conversation with someone. As I looked closer, I could tell she was discouraged. With her play cell phone in one hand and her other hand on her hips, mouth poked out, she was mad! It was really cute, and I couldn't help but intrude. "Hi, honey, who are you talking to?" She looked at me, lowering her big brown eyes as she began to tell me that the person she was calling kept hanging up on her!

I couldn't help but chuckle on the inside because this precious baby really believed she was talking to a person on a toy cell phone and this person was choosing to hang up on her. I probed further. "Well, who were you talking to?" Without hesitation she said, "God!"

I couldn't control my laughter any longer. "Oh baby, God wouldn't hang up on you." She pushed the phone into my hand and said, "Um hum. Listen." I took the phone from her and pretended to talk with God. "Hello, hello, God—yes, how are

You? Well, this little girl I'm looking at said You hung up on her. I didn't think so. Hold on, here she is."

I handed the phone back to the little girl who now had a big smile on her face. Anxiously awaiting her turn to talk to God, brown eyes now bright and little hands waving as if to say, "Hurry up and give it to me! I'm ready to talk to God." She was delighted; we now had a connection!

With headset in place and a smile on her face she demanded, "God, why You keep hanging up on me?!" As quickly as the smile appeared, it was gone. Her mouth returned to the pout, and her brown eyes dropped simultaneously with the phone as she spoke with a sigh, "He hung up again!"

Yep. That little girl was just like me! It always seemed as if God talked to select adults and my Granny, but He didn't talk to us kids! As I got older, I realized that you don't need a phone to contact God when He's living inside you in the Person of Holy Spirit!! If you've confessed Jesus as Lord of your life, He does live on the inside of you in the person of Holy Spirit. If you haven't confessed Jesus as Lord, you can wait until you finish reading this book, or turn to the section at the back of the book titled, "A Letter of Recommendation," and you can be saved now right where you are!

Once I began to realize who God was and began to fellowship with Him, I discovered I didn't feel "comfortable" talking to Him. After all, why would the God who created the earth, made man, lived in heaven, and had angels bow down and worship Him at His throne, talk to me? The idea was hard for me to comprehend. I was thinking too much and not reading enough of my Bible. The Bible is full of Scriptures that tell about the love of God for you, how He wants to commune with you, that He expects praise from you as we discussed earlier. Carol

If you aren't talking to God, He is talking to you. I know now that God talks to children *and* adults; they just confuse Him with their "conscience" and the "something told me" person. "You know . . Something told me to call my son's teacher." "Something told me to buy my wife some flowers." Stop calling Holy Spirit "something." Yes, there could be several voices talking to you at one time—the voice of God in the Person of Holy Spirit, your own voice, and the voice of the enemy. You need to know who's speaking to you! Attend a good Bible church and get information. Don't be like the little girl on the cell phone—God *is* talking to you. He's not hanging up on you. You just don't know how to listen.

The more you talk to God, the more you'll *want* to talk to Him. First, He's good at keeping secrets. He won't tell anyone else what you've said. After all, God sent Jesus to redeem you and Holy Spirit to live and dwell inside you to be your Best Friend. He will help you. Holy Spirit gives you life-changing insight. He'll give you a God idea.

During times of fellowship with God, I try to be very honest and straightforward with Him. Don't try to fool yourself or God. He knows your heart and what you're thinking. You can't continue to pretend that you're having a great time with Him when you're not. He's not like people. You can't fake it with Him.

Begin talking to God on a consistent basis and what a change in your life you'll see! Don't leave out Holy Spirit; He's a wonderful Friend who will talk to you at any time. Go ahead, put the book down and ask Him. Say this, "Is it true, will You talk to me now Holy Spirit? Is there something You want to say?" Don't you be a "chicken" as the adults used to tell me when I was afraid to do something. Once you ask, listen for a still, quiet voice. Go ahead, start up a conversation and begin to enjoy your new Friend!

Dare To Know All About God

My sheep hear my voice, and I know them, and they follow me:

John 10:27

This particular Scripture in my Bible is written in red, which means Jesus Himself spoke these words. He said we would know His voice and that He would know ours and we would follow Him. You get to know someone's voice when you hear it often, which means you must hang around them. My children can be in a crowd of people, but if they are talking, I can pick them out. Many of you can do the same with your loved ones. You know your husband's voice, your wife's, and your friends. Hang around God long enough, talk to Him, and you'll get to know His voice.

After you start talking to God, you will get to know Him and His character. He's not the mean Ogre, as some of you were raised to believe. He's a Sweetie full of mercy and grace; a wonderful Savior to be respected and reverenced; God of glory, worthy of praise. He is the Holy One, our Anchor. He's faithful Father and Friend. As your Father, He can, and will, bring correction, when needed.

Knowing God for yourself will help you praise Him. I remember one day while praising God, I could feel His presence and it was oh so sweet. I was expressing to Him how good it felt to seek

Him earnestly and verbalize what was in my heart. I began to sing a song taken from a wonderful Broadway musical *The King and I*, written by Rodgers and Hammerstein. The song is called "Getting to Know You." I couldn't put the lyrics here because of copyright infringement laws. But I had a great time singing this song, even though I was singing the wrong words and making up my own. But because I felt the urge to serenade the Lord, I went on the internet to find the correct words. When I found them, I began to dance and sing and jump around, because I was so excited that I was "Getting to Know God" for myself. For once, I was expressing my love to Him and the words were mine -- all mine. There was nothing really "spiritual" about our time together. I was just happy being in His presence having Him all to myself.

God wants our hearts. He is not interested in us saying all the right things, when in our hearts we're saying or feeling something else. Isaiah 29:13 in the Amplified Bible says, *"And the Lord said, Forasmuch as this people draw near Me with their mouth and honor Me with their lips but remove their hearts and minds far from Me, and their fear and reverence for Me are a commandment of men that is learned by repetition [without any thought as to the meaning]."* Wow, let's look at Matthew 15:8 in the Amplified as well, *"These people draw near Me with their mouths and honor Me with their lips, but their hearts hold off and are far away from Me."* Let's not be like the people referred to in these passages of Scripture. When we praise God, let it come from our heart and flow from our lips.

Did God care that the song I was singing to Him didn't come from a hymn book? I don't think so. I believe He had a smile on His face because I was praising and worshipping Him from my heart. Like a child, I was dancing before Him uninhibited by religion and other folks.

Perhaps your experience with God is much different from what mine used to be. I didn't even know if God *liked* me. When I was young, both in age and in the things of God, I knew He loved me, somehow; but you can love people and not like them because of what they do. For example, if your fifteen-year-old goes shopping with you and decides to go down the clothing aisle and throw all the clothes on the floor, you wouldn't like your teenager at that moment. You'd still love them, but you would dislike their actions.

I discovered that God not only liked me, He loved me. I found out I was the apple of His eye. Really, I am, and so are you. Look it up for yourself if you don't believe me. (Deuteronomy 32:10 and Psalms 17:18)

I had been told so many lies about God earlier in my Christian walk. After reading the Bible for myself, I discovered that those things I had been told were misconstrued by me and the persons relating the information to me. God had been misrepresented. As you read about Him, talk to Him and fellowship with Him—praise Him. When you praise and love Him because you know Him for yourself, your praise will be true and from your heart.

When I was "getting to know God," I had a difficult time "cutting down all the weeds of religion." I felt like I was in a jungle cutting down bush. For example, people always told me what I couldn't do when serving God, but the Bible is full of can do's. They told me that God would strike me down, but I'm finding that He wants to lift me up. I've heard about God being the harsh Judge, but if you judge yourself you won't have to be judged by Him (I Corinthians 11:31).

Ask yourself these questions: When was the last time you boasted about God? Which do you do more of—boasting, complaining, or asking? If you became an expert at praising God and fellowshipping with Holy Spirit, what would that do to your relationship with Him? Is He the subject you like most? Is He even close? Do you want to know about Him? What steps are you taking?

Do you really *like* God? Have you disliked God, because someone told you your loved one died because God "needed another flower?" God does not need to kill someone for another flower. If He can make a man and keep the sun in the sky, all He has to say is "flower be" and it will appear. God does not kill people for flowers or because He needs another angel. I know sometimes people say that. Most don't mean it in the literal sense, but you'd be surprised, some do and that's an insult to God and hurtful to the deceased relatives who are left to mourn.

If someone else hasn't shown you the Word of God on this subject, then get a Bible and go to John 10:10, it reads, *"The thief cometh not, but for to steal, and to kill, and to destroy: I am come that they might have life, and that they might have it more abundantly."*

Another Scripture, James 1:17 puts it this way, *"Every good gift and every perfect gift is from above, and cometh down from the Father of lights, with whom there is no variableness, neither shadow of turning."*

You can learn to like God—He's magnificent! John 3:16 tells us that God loves us so much that He gave His Son Jesus to die for us. *You don't do that for people you don't like!* And you don't hang around people you don't like. Holy Spirit is your hanging Buddy; I'd say that He really likes you! I have three children, and I can't think of one person including my brothers and sisters that I would sacrifice my children for! It wouldn't happen!

You want a good stress reliever? Try spending some time in the presence of God. The next time you find yourself praising God, before you leave His presence, ask Him. "Lord, show or tell me something beautiful about You that I don't know. I really want to learn all I can." If He doesn't tell you right then, keep listening, keep looking around. He'll reveal something that you didn't previously know or see. No one can know all that there is to know about God, and we probably never will. He's too big. But if you're truly interested (and He'll know), He will share wonderful, beautiful things with you. Watch and see! He's done it for me, and He'll do it for you!

Some of us may respect and fear God, but don't feel we can say we love Him, because we are afraid of God. We're scared that He is going to "get us," because of the thoughts and things we do that He doesn't like. That's why it used to be difficult for me to say, "I love You, Lord," and mean it from my heart. I said it—because it was expected. But what I *voiced* and *felt* were contrary to each other like the Scripture we read earlier from Matthew 15:8. Why was what I voiced different than what I felt? It was because I really didn't know God.

Once I made a decision to get lost in my praise, I realized that I had a huge advantage. I had a Helper who not only knew God, but He is the Third Person of the Godhead—Holy Spirit! And help you He will, but you must be willing to talk with Him to find out how!

God has given us so many tools to help us study His Word and know all about Him. When reading His Word, you will learn how He feels about you. And after you learn about Him all the days of your life, you still won't exhaust all that's in the Bible.

Like me, you too can sing the "Getting to Know You" song to God. God does not care that it came from *The King and I*. After all, in reality, it's you and the King! You may come up with something wilder than that. Surely, when you get caught up praising God,

Holy Spirit will cause you to sing sweet songs of praise, and, if you don't know a lot, you'll be surprised at what God will let you use to praise Him, once you dare to know Him.

Elevate Your Praise

Because thy loving kindness is better than life, my lips shall praise thee. Thus will I bless thee while I live: I will lift up my hands in thy name.

Psalms 63:3–4

Lift up your hands in the sanctuary, and bless the Lord.

Psalms 134:2

While I was vacationing in San Francisco, the Lord revealed to me that He wanted me to write this book. I awoke one morning and walked around the Bay praying and praising God. The scenery was picture-perfect. Surrounded by dancing water on both sides and lush greens, I felt God's presence like never before. The only sound was that of birds singing. I was thanking God for providing the resources for the vacation and praising Him for a job well done. Palm trees swinging in the breeze, boats floating in the bay, the wind gently embracing my skin, what a beautiful sight to behold.

Then, as usual, I began to praise God using what I call the *"ABC's of Praise."* I was thanking Holy Spirit for teaching me how to love God, when I heard Him whisper to me, "I want you to put this in a book." What a surprise to me! I then asked, "Put this in a book? Me? Why?" Holy Spirit then told me that "the personal experiences and concerns you have regarding praise are shared by others, and they are seeking help, as well, in entering praise." It was further revealed that the principles I use to go to another level of praise will help those who truly want to "raise their praise" to God, without being clock-watchers.

Holy Spirit told me in order to increase my praise, I needed to do something I had never done before. He said, "Begin with the letter A and go through the alphabet to Z declaring with each letter of the alphabet the goodness of God or my feelings about God." Well, the first time was pretty easy. As I began to do it the second time, Holy Spirit said, "This time do not use any religious terms like Alpha and Omega, the Beginning and End, King of kings, Holy God, God of Mercy, God of Grace, God of Love, Hallelujah." It still wasn't too difficult until I got to the Q, X, Y, and Z. Those were the letters I got stuck on.

After about three or four times of doing this Holy Spirit added another level. He said, "I now want you to pull out the dictionary and find words to express your love and gratitude to God starting with A going through the alphabet to Z." I got out a notebook and labeled the pages A through Z. As I perused the dictionary, I wrote words that expressed to me who God was and how I felt toward Him, His Son, and Holy Spirit.

This was an exercise I would do over and over, using the dictionary as my resource, so I wouldn't get stuck. That's why it's called the *ABC's of Praise*.

Depending on your background you might be asking yourself, "Why does the author keep saying Holy Spirit said this and Holy Spirit said that?" When Jesus returned to heaven after rising from the dead, He didn't leave us to fend for ourselves. In John 14:16–17 Jesus says, *"And I will pray the Father, and he shall give you another Comforter, that he may abide with you forever; Even the Spirit of truth; whom the world cannot receive, because it seeth him not, neither knoweth him: but ye know him; for he dwelleth with you, and shall be in you.* " John 14:26 says, *"But the Comforter, which is the Holy Ghost, whom the Father will send in my name, he shall teach you all things and bring all things to your remembrance, whatsoever I have said unto you. "*

I want those of you who have confessed Jesus as Lord to know that you are blessed with the Person of Holy Spirit. He is your Comforter who is always with you, because He lives inside you. He's a Teacher and Reminder. He will help you recall things. He's the Third Person of the Godhead. Holy Spirit should be so real to you that if you were by yourself and passed gas or belched, you would say, "Excuse me, Holy Spirit."

Once I realized Holy Spirit was a person, I started treating Him like one. The more you acknowledge Him and talk to Him, the greater the relationship.

Although this is not a teaching on Holy Spirit, you should know who you have on the inside. To me, praise is "loving on God" by telling Him "Who He is to you, and how much you love and honor Him by telling Him how grateful you are for Him."

I didn't know how to do it naturally, but the Person who is always with me has known God since He was. What better Person to teach me how to love Him than someone Who's been with Him for eternity! And Holy Spirit will help you with your *ABC's of Praise.*

You will no longer continue, year after year, to say the same things to God. "Hallelujah, Hallelujah, Glory to God, Glory to Your Name. I love You, Lord, I love You, Lord. You are good. You are good." Yes, God is all of these, but wouldn't you like to add something to that? He's too big, too wonderful not to venture out and tell Him something different about Himself that you adore. Please don't misunderstand me—at times, especially during a worship service (or at home), you will still, even after practicing the *ABC's of Praise*, find yourself saying certain words or phrases repeatedly. It's okay to tell the Lord over and over how much you love Him. But find different ways to say it. He's a BIG God and we need to take the limits off our praise.

Go the extra mile for God and expand your praise vocabulary. When you do, wonderful things will begin to happen for you. Enlarge your praise tent. Write praise in the form of a letter. Or write Him a song or poem.

Buy a special notebook for praise and begin by spending five minutes on each letter of the alphabet. After you write about ten words under each letter, begin to think about what you want to say to God. If it's on a day when everything is beautiful, then you might want to pen praise on how magnificent God is. Maybe it's not a good day— your check is gone, and you haven't even touched the bills you need to pay; then your praise might be on the line of Jesus being your Provider despite what you see. In the midst of this temporary lack, He is still worthy of praise. No matter how bad things seem, you can always find something to be thankful for, if you truly desire to praise the Lord.

One day as I was praising God, I started with A and the word I used was "*appreciate*." I was telling the Lord how much I appreciated His faithfulness, and in my spirit, a light went on. I stopped in the middle of my praise and thought: How many words can I find that mean the same thing as "*appreciate?*"

I pulled out some of my resources *(Webster's Concise English Thesaurus and The Writer's Digest Flip Dictionary)* and this is what I found under **appreciate:** admire, adore, enjoy, esteem, gain, give thanks to, grateful, hold in high regard, increase, judge, like, love, recognize, respect, take pleasure in, thankful, treasure, understand, value, welcome.

I had a field day praising the Lord on that one word alone. I went crazy giving God praise. One word can become a whole praise when you go that extra mile. You will "raise your praise" by just using the word *appreciate.* Here's what I wrote:

> Father, yes, I *appreciate* You. Men *admire* many things, but I have someone I can *admire* who won't let me down. That someone is You, Daddy. I admire the way Your Son, in obedience, went to the cross for me.
>
> You're my hero, Jesus. I *adore* You and everything about You. I *enjoy* being in Your presence. Your company is sweet. I *esteem* You more than anything. I *gain* from being in Your presence. I *gain* strength, courage, peace. You name it, I *gain* it.
>
> I *give thanks to* You for never quitting on me. I thank You for the precious Blood. I thank You for another day. I'm *grateful* for what You've done for me in spite of myself. I *hold in high regard* Your Word that changes my life. I *increase* in my spirit every time I'm in Your presence.
>
> *Judging* from all I know about You, I would not want to live without You. You Three are Men of integrity. I *like* communing with You. I reap revelation, confidence, and encouragement when we hang out. I *love* You with all my heart, my soul, my very being.
>
> I *recognize* that nobody, nowhere, with clout and status, would put up with me. But You God

Almighty, embrace me with open arms. I **respect** everything about You. How You set standards and even abide by Your own standards.

I **take pleasure in** the fact of knowing that You don't operate on hearsay. You know me, You make Yourself available to me at all times. I take pleasure in knowing that You will never leave me. I'm so **thankful**. There are not enough words to express how thankful I am to You!

I **treasure** You more than silver, gold, or relationships. Those things are subject to change, but You will always be here with me. I **understand** what I've been blessed with. Having You as my Father, Jesus as my Lord and Big Brother, and Holy Spirit as my Friend, I need nothing else.

My **value** is increased just because I know You and because of the Name You've given me, the Name of Jesus! Every other name is below that Name and will bow to the Name of Jesus. I **welcome** You during this time of praise because I know what I have in You! Glory to God!

I just wrote that from my heart using the word **appreciate**. How do you think our Father feels when His children take time to love Him like that! We're not in a hurry. We'll do whatever it takes to convey to Him with clarity how we feel. I think He'll be quite pleased.

As you can see, I started with one word—**appreciate**. The thesaurus rendered seventeen additional words and three phrases.

Now log these words in your notebook for future praise under the correct letter. Each day, build on what you have. Not only did you receive one word for the letter *A* when you looked up that word in the thesaurus, you can now log all the other seventeen words and three phrases we just talked about.

After you write your feelings on paper, and you're satisfied with the way it reads, go to the next step. Close the thesaurus and shut out any other thoughts. Stand and lift your hands and read your praise to the Lord out loud and boldly proclaim what you were able to pen, after some thought. Be creative and spontaneous. Being free in your praise is wonderful, and this is only the beginning.

I've already told you about my frustrations and inability to communicate my praise to God, but I had another issue as well: raising my hands. In the worship service, I lifted my hands to God like I was scared. My wrist was flipped up, so it gave the appearance that my hand was raised but my elbows were bent clutching my side. I felt so uncomfortable that I would look around to see if anyone was watching me.

Let's look at hand-raising a little further. When you want to be heard in a crowded room, or get the attention of the person in charge, you don't yell and say, "Hey, I want to talk." No, out of respect for their position, you raise your hand.

If you're in a fight and you decide to "surrender," you hold up your hands and begin to walk toward the one you're surrendering. When you are at a sporting event and your team makes a great shot, or someone does something extraordinary, you stand up, thrust your hands in the air, and yell "Yay!" Or you lift your hands in the air with clenched fists as a sign of "victory."

When I enter into the presence of the "One in charge of my life," out of respect to Him, I lift my hands. When I realize that I can't "fight the good fight of faith" without surrendering to God, I raise my hands in surrender. When I think about the winning team I'm on and all the extraordinary things that Jesus has done and is still doing, I lift my hands and say, "Yay—You be the Man!" When I come into the presence of the King, I honor Him by raising my hands in total awe of Who He is and the victory He has provided for me! Scripture tells us to come into the presence of the Lord lifting holy hands. (1 Timothy 2:8) So, lift those holy hands unto the Lord!

During my change from no praise to limited praise to where I am now, I remember an incident in the sanctuary that brought about another change regarding lifting my hands. I was lifting my arms during a praise song (I had not yet graduated to doing it at home), and my arms got tired after about half a minute into the song. They got so tired that I had to rest them by putting them down for a while. This bothered me. Here I was enjoying the praise, raising my arms and hands to the Lord, and my *flesh* made me put my hands down. I made the decision then that I would do something about it. If I decided to lower my hands during praise, it would be because I got a release in my spirit and not because of my flesh telling me my arms were tired!

I immediately began to wonder how I could strengthen my arms so I could hold them up as long as *I* wanted! One day while I was on my exercise bike, Holy Spirit told me to begin to "exercise my arms and strengthen them." What a revelation! You probably figured that out by yourself, but I needed help from my Helper.

I began to do arm exercises at home to build my arms. I wasn't exercising for myself, I was exercising for the mission that nothing would hinder my praise. I was determined to go the extra mile in every area so I wouldn't be forced to lower my arms because I was tired. I bet Jesus was tired of having His arms stretched out on the cross, but He hung there anyway determined to complete His assignment to redeem us. If Jesus could hang on the cross for my sins, surely, I could keep my hands raised for the entire praise song *if I wanted to*! With arms extended to the side, I would begin moving my hands in a circular motion: 1, 2, 3, 4, 5, 6, 7, 8, 9, 10. Then I would repeat the cycle with my hands going in the reverse direction: 1, 2, 3, 4, 5, 6, 7, 8, 9, 10. This was one complete cycle. I continued doing this until I had worked myself up to five cycles for a total of one hundred circles.

Next, I began to work on the horizontal motion. I extended my arms upward, palms facing the ceiling. Then, I would paddle my arms like riding a bike. I can't tell you how many of these I did, but I kept doing them until my arms were strengthened enough to hold them up as long as *I* wanted! My flesh was not going to tell me, "You can put your hands down if you're tired, God will understand!" No! I was determined to raise my hands to God until *I* felt released to let them down.

I'm not trying to tell you how long you should raise your hands to God—that's between you and God. But as you grow in your praise (and it takes time), you should increase in every area. I'm only sharing these things with you because again, if these were areas I struggled with, I know someone reading this book is feeling the same. I also know sharing what I went through will help you get delivered sooner than later.

However, if you don't feel comfortable in God's presence, your praise will not reach the level you desire. When I first began to praise, I didn't understand why God wanted me (a little nobody) to bestow accolades to Him. But shouldn't I tell Him what a great job He did creating the earth? Shouldn't I give Him compliments on the different trees? The beautiful flowers, too many to number. How about the various animals, their shapes and sizes? The beauty in them all. Shouldn't I tell Him what a great job He's done!!

After discovering how much God loves me and realizing that I am somebody because God said so, I understood why He wanted a relationship with me that included praise. I wanted to honor God.

Jesus has made things so easy for us, and I think sometimes we get too complacent with God. Because we have access to the Father, if we're not careful, our relationship becomes common. Instead of getting up for praying or praising, if it's cold with a lot of snow outside, we lie in the bed. I did it *once too often* and my Helper checked me. Holy Spirit said to me, "If the President walked into the room right now, would you lie in the bed and say, 'Hey, Mr. President.'" No. If I knew the President was coming, I would get up, brush my teeth, comb my hair, and look like I was expecting royalty. Holy Spirit said, "You need to do that sometimes for the Lord—He's become too common to you." Wow, that jerked the slack out of me. Do I do this every time? No. But still at times I get on my knees before honoring and praising God. Sometimes I spruce myself up by combing my hair, dabbing on some perfume, and putting on something nice before ministering to God in the privacy of my home—why? Because He is God, and He deserves my best.

Don't get so comfortable with God that you forget who He is. It's true He doesn't care how, or what, you look like, but if you dress up for your boyfriend or spouse, and God blessed you with them—dress up for Him sometimes too. Don't let Holy Spirit remind you that the last time you were on your knees you were looking for a shoe under your bed. Get on your knees for Him. Then, with a smile on your face, hold up your arms while on your knees and say, "Lord, I bow before You today in honor and respect of Who You are. I just want to love You and give reverence on my knees."

If what I've just said agrees with your spirit, make sure you act on it.

THE FATHER IS WAITING JUST FOR YOU

I will sing unto the Lord as long as I live: I will sing praise to my God while I have my being.

Psalms 104:33

There are many ways to use the *ABC's of Praise*. Sometimes, I'll use the same letter more than once. Don't limit yourself in how you use this principle. Be free to express to God how you feel. You can start by praying and just begin to praise Him. Start with G and go through Z. Or begin with A and go through G.

For your first try, do not use any of the praise language that you've used before (i.e., I love You, Lord; Glory, Hallelujah). Your praise won't be like mine, so don't try to put sentences together. Just say the letter of the alphabet and choose a corresponding praise. Keep your first one simple. Write down what comes to mind or use a dictionary if necessary. Remember, your word to the corresponding alphabet letter should remind you of the Lord and His faithfulness, His lovingkindness, and His goodness. You can cheat by asking Holy Spirit to help you (smile). In the beginning, always start with A and say something like this . . .

Lord, I stand before You, bursting with praise, and I want You to know that I **Applaud** You for the many times You've extended Your grace to me. Without You my life would be out of **Balance**. I praise You, for being my **Champion**. I praise You for coming to my **Defense** when no one else would.

Before you begin to use the *ABC's of Praise*, I want you to confess what follows. It's not a praise, just a confession to build your confidence as you start your journey. I only used the *ABC's of Praise* format to write the confession. If you remember these twenty-six things (they will build your confidence), you will achieve your desire to "raise your praise and get lost in Him." You may need to refer to them, so bookmark this page in advance. Make sure you read the alphabet first, then what comes after.

Father, when I think about "raising my praise and getting lost in You.. "
A- lets me know that You are **Approachable**.
B- assures me that I can **Build** on our relationship.
C- reminds me that You **Chose** me first.
D- lets me know that this will not be **Difficult.**
E- says that I'm going to **Enjoy** this!
F- tells me to not **Faint** in the process.
G- reminds me that my **Goal** is to **Grow** in praise!
H- says that **Holy Spirit** will help me learn to praise You.
I- will allow me to **Imagine** how wonderful You are.
J- declares the **Journey** will be sweet.
K- You are the **Key** to my success, and You deserve the honor.
L- I won't **Limit** my resources in my quest to raise my praise.
M- I'll **Make** the adjustment to spend time to praise You.
N- I'll no longer be **Narrow** in my thinking regarding praise.
O- You have **Opened** the door to great and wonderful things.
P- I'm going to **Proceed** with a vengeance!

Q- I won't **Quit** praising You—**EVER!**

R- I **Refuse** to give up!

S- I'll no longer be **Satisfied** with my praise as it is now.

T- This is a new and **Thrilling** experience!

U- I'm expecting **Unusual** fellowship with You.

V- My praise will **Virtually** be revolutionized.

W- I **Want** so much for You to be pleased.

X- Your **X-ray** vision into my heart confirms my sincerity.

Y- I **Yearn** to go higher in my praise.

Z- I'm **Zany** about You and I'm not ashamed to say so.

If you remember what's written above, you will be successful in raising your praise.

It's your turn now. Go through the alphabet and think of ways to praise the Lord. I've already put the letters in place at the end of this section. If you need to, go to a dictionary, but be determined to get your praise on. If possible, try really hard to do it on your own the first couple of times, without help from outside sources. Let me warn you that Q, V, X, Y, and Z will take a lot of imagination, but you have Holy Spirit, your Helper. You'll be amazed at what He will teach you about loving God!

You will get better with practice. The best part is that while doing this, your thought life will be totally focused on the Lord. Go ahead, write your first *ABC's of Praise,* and then don't forget to lift your hands after you write it and speak it out loud to the Lord.

A= _____

B= _____

C= _____

D= _____

E= _____

F= _____

G= _____

H= _____

I= _____

J= _____

K= _____

L= _____

M= _____

N= _____

O= _____

P= _____

Q= _____

R= _____

S= _____

T= _____

U= _____

V= _____

W= _____

X= _____

Y= _____

Z= _____

Go ahead, try another one.

A= _____

B= _____

C= _____

D= _____

E= _____

F= _____

G= _____

H= _____

I= _____

J= _____

K= _____

L= _____

M= _____

N= _____

O= _____

P= _____

Q= _____

R= _____

S= _____

T= _____

U= _____

V= _____

W= _____

X= _____

Y= _____

Z= _____

Very good!

Go For It!

Let my mouth be filled with thy praise and with thy honor all the day.

Psalms 71:8

Now that you've learned the ABC concept, let's write some more. I'm going to teach you various ways to praise; later you can add your own. I'll show you how to apply the *ABC's of Praise* using mostly *biblical terms*. Later, we'll do "strictly from the heart;" we'll get *r e a l* serious, and we can't and won't leave out a fun one. I'm even going to show you how to praise using negative circumstances—yeah! And you'll have more opportunities to write your own praise. Remember, our purpose is to think about God and all that He is, so much so that we aren't thinking about doing the dishes, cooking dinner, presenting a work project, cutting the grass, or shoveling the snow.

The ABC's of Praise, if done correctly, will again block out everything else that's vying for your attention so you can quickly "get lost in Him." Let's begin by praising using familiar terms. Read the following praise from *A* to *Z*, then read it again really praising God as Holy Spirit prompts you.

Lord Jesus, I lift my hands to You today, to honor You and all that You are and for what You've done. The **A**tonement for my sins was enough, but You didn't stop there. You gave me Your written Word, in the form of a **B**ible, that feeds me spiritual food, nourishing my body. **C**alvary was not a pretty picture, but You went there anyway, just for me, where You bore every **D**isease so that I wouldn't have to. What an awesome God You are! Because of the cross, You made available to me **E**ternal Life. You're so wonderful. Your mercy and grace are infinite. You **F**orgive me when I sin, and promised in Your Word that You would remove my transgressions as far as the East is from the West. You amaze me with Your patience.

Just thinking about You, my hands go up and I say "**G**lory." You are a **H**oly God, and because of You, I can be holy too. After all, I've been made in Your **I**mage and **J**ustified. Truly You are **K**ing of kings and Lord of lords. You were the innocent **L**amb that was slain for my sins. Jesus, You are the great **M**ediator. Your **N**ame is above all names, and one day every knee will bow, and every tongue will confess that You are Lord. Oh, how I love You—You made an **O**ath, swore by it, and that covenant still stands today. You are not like a man that You would go back on Your **O**ath, but I can depend on Your Word. I'm no longer **P**ressed like I used to be. I lift my hands to You, oh Lord, for You have done marvelous things! My spirit has been **Q**uieted like a child being rocked to sleep in his mother's arms.

My **R**edeemer, oh how I adore You. You **S**acrificed Yourself and emerged **T**riumphant. Thank You for Your **U**nfailing love. Thank You for being a Giver. My **V**ision is no longer blurred. You give joy, peace, mercy, and wisdom, and I **W**orship You. To say that You are **X**-tra large is an insult because You are bigger than life, **Y**ahweh. Thank You for being the covenant-keeping God. If

Zion can sing because You dwell in the midst of it, so will I sing of Your goodness because You're in my midst as well.

Yes, God is all of the above and more. That's why we must expand our praise. He's too big—we must stretch ourselves when it comes to praising Him.

Here's another warm-up using familiar biblical terms. Remember though, as we get further, we'll branch out into the nontraditional praise, but it will all glorify God. Your praise will take you to higher levels. No longer will your praise be repetitive and mundane because you don't have anything else to say; you'll branch out and give God your best. Get ready to put your praise on . . .

Father, I praise You because You are **A**lmighty God. There is no other God but You. Thank You for the **B**lood shed by Your Son Jesus on the **C**ross at **C**alvary that I might be free from sin, sickness, and spiritual death. I praise You for the **C**ovenant that I have with You, one that has been in place since my great, great, great grandfather Abraham. You swore by it then and it still applies to me now. You have always been my **D**eliverer, setting me free from the traps that the enemy set for me, and, when I listen to You, You keep me from ever stepping into those traps.

You are my **E**xample of how I should live and have given me Your Word. You have been a **F**aithful **F**ather, One I can depend on in every situation, One who has never **F**ailed me. I will **G**lorify Your Name forevermore. I have the most precious **G**ift anyone could ever have in the Person of **H**oly Spirit, Who is a Friend and comfort to me. I am **I**nsatiable (I can't get enough of) with You!

Thank You for being **J**ehovah God. I can call on You anytime I need You because You are the One who's always there. There are no **K**inks in Your plan! Your **L**eadership is impeccable. Not only are You a **M**erciful God, but You're the **M**ost High God!

Thank You Lord, that my **N**ame is written in the "Lamb's Book of Life." Your ears are always **O**pen to hear me when I call. You **P**romised You would never leave nor forsake me— and in this I have confidence. When I think about all that You are, my mind becomes **Q**uiet, and I can again **R**est and know that I'm **S**afe in Your arms.

Thank You for being my **T**eacher, Holy Spirit. You guide me into all **T**ruth, helping me to **U**nderstand the Father and Jesus's Love for me. My lips shall **U**tter praise, as I learn from God's statutes, which help me live free from sin. I **V**ow to love and **W**orship You Lord all the days of my life.

You are the **X** that causes blessings to be multiplied in my life. **Y**ou, oh God, are my everything! I would be a big fat **Z**ero without You!

When you begin to praise God like this, you will see that because all your efforts are used in thinking about Who He is, and what you're going to say, your mind can't wander on to other things. Thus, you get lost in ministering to God!

By the way, according to *The New Strong's Exhaustive Concordance of the Bible*, I only found one word that began with *X* in the King James Bible. That word is Xerxes, it refers to King Ahasuerus, who God used to save the Jews. You can read about him in The Book of Esther. Therefore, we must be creative and use other words that can be described by *X* such as "multiply."

STRICTLY FROM THE HEART

*I will praise thee, O Lord, with my whole heart; I will
shew forth all thy marvelous works.*

Psalms 9:1

Sometimes, you want to just pour out your heart to God. You'll
have one of those days when people disappoint you and God comes
through, where you know that if not for Him, you wouldn't know
what to do. You'll find yourself with such a feeling of gratitude
and thanksgiving that all you want to do is tell God how much
you love and care for Him. When you feel like that, one letter
won't do. You will use double, triple, and quadruple letters of the
same alphabet.

The ABC's of Praise is like a bridge that will connect you to
God *right away.* This particular praise is just what the title says:
Strictly From The Heart. I want you to read it first, then reflect on
your day. If it applies, once again after you read it, lift your hand,
and verbalize it to the Lord. If you want to change anything or,
if Holy Spirit brings something to mind, remember this is your
book. Get a pen or pencil and insert what's in your heart. Together
let's give God some praise…

Lord—today I want to express from my heart
how much You mean to me. It amazes me how

You **Always Arrange** Your time around mine. Never could I accuse You of being an **Absent** God. Thank You for being **Actively** involved in my life. You never, ever tell me You are too **Busy** to talk with me. It **Boggles** the mind. After all, You are the God who created the heavens and earth. You're magnificent, yet You're always there for me. Even when I **Babble** about what's **Bothering** me, You never **Brush** me off or tell me to "get to the point!" You are **Capable** of handling my problems and those in **China** at the same time. I'm so **Comfortable** around You. Your love **Carries** me when I'm weak and beat-up. You are a **Colossal** God. I can **Depend** on You even when I know that I've wronged someone, including You. You're so worthy of praise. How can I withhold it from You! I won't, I can't. You're so special to me.

You've caused broken **Dreams** to come to pass. **Disappointments** that I never thought I could recover from, You've found a way to **Ease** my pain. Your **Ear** is always open to hear my cry. How **Excellent** are You, oh God!

If only I would learn to seek You first before I take on projects, life would be much **Easier**. You've said You would lead and guide me, and every time I've sought You, never once have You gone back on Your Word. What a God of integrity You are!

Faithful Father, how much **Fairer** can You be? Your Word says to seek **You First, in the morning and evening**. You're so **Generous** with Your blessings. Your **G**entle voice wakes me every morning. I have sense enough to know that it is not the alarm clock. You **G**ive me bread to eat. You provide spiritual, physical, and financial **G**rowth in my life. When I ask, You provide **G**uidance and even when I don't, Your **G**race sustains me, and You still lead me in the right direction. I would be out of my mind to not praise such a worthy **G**od!

I have a **H**ome, thanks to You. You've provided **H**eat in the winter. You've broken **H**abits, and caused me to be joint **H**eir with You. You've never been **I**cy with me. Your warmth is so **I**nviting. I never **I**magined that it could be this good between us. You have never **I**solated Yourself from me, which causes my **J**ourney to be so much easier. I've never had to **J**ump through hoops to be with You. I'm **J**oined with You forever, and that makes me feel so secure.

Jesus, thank You for being my High Priest and going to the Father on my behalf. You're too good to me!

You have **K**ept me. Your **K**indness goes beyond anything I can imagine. I never have to worry about You **K**icking me to the curb. You'll never give up on me because of Your **L**ove. Lessons **L**earned in the past sometimes are still hindrances keeping me from my today, preventing me from getting to my tomorrow. How can I forget the **M**esses I've gotten myself into; You've **M**anaged to get me out of them all, even though I know I'm still responsible for what I've done. You are right in the Middle, telling me I can make it. You and I are a Majority, what comfort.

I have Someone on my side who is not afraid of anything, and that Someone is You, oh Lord. Before our relationship, I thought I knew what I could and could not live without. I've found out that the One Person Necessary in my life is You. Nothing is too hard or difficult for You. I no longer have to be beat up by the enemy and people. Nay, in all things I am not just a conqueror, Your Word says I am more than a conqueror; and since You said it, that settles it.

Overwhelmed—only when I neglect to focus on You! My Opportunities to walk in Your blessings have increased. Your Word has caused my eyes to Open and see Your goodness. You, oh God, have Peeled away doubt, unbelief, and fear. Nobody but You Picked me up when I was so low, I thought I could not make it. Bless the Name of the Lord—You are marvelous! You have become the Problem Solver in my life. I never Question Your commitment to me. Before I really came to know You, I was a Quitter. Now, I've become a fighter. I don't give up, and thanks to You I win. You've caused critics to be Quieted. You've Restored Relationships, and things that mean so much to me. I must admit that there are times in my life where You are the only Reason I can Rise out of bed. You help me Recover when the world says I'm going under. I am **S**afe in Your arms. I am **S**trengthened by Your presence. I am **S**teady in my walk. I praise You for being my **S**trong tower—I can run to You and find **S**afety. Oh, how I adore You!

You've set this thing up so that I can **T**alk to You whenever I please, and I'm grateful for it. Thank You, Lord, I don't have to go through a secretary to get time with You. . .I always have Your ear. With Your help, I've **T**orn down strongholds; my skin has become **T**hick. Words that other people say don't hurt as much because of You. I'm no longer **T**errified of what the devil can do; because You've given me a Friend who **T**ravels with me everywhere I go, that would be Holy Spirit. With You on my side, and Holy Spirit in me, what can man do to me? Nothing!

Any praise I render to You is **U**nderstated because of Your greatness. I don't **U**nderstand all there is to You but this I know, You do love me, You do care for me, You do protect me, You do provide for me. You cause me to have the **U**pper hand in every situation. **U**ncommon is Your love, and I'm glad that You loved me first. Oh yeah, You **V**olunteered to love me—nobody forced You or paid You, it was a **V**oluntary act. You saw me in my sinful state and still chose me.

Only after I tried in **V**ain to fill a **V**oid, You filled that **V**acant spot that no other could fill. You told me from Your Word how **V**aluable I was.

My **V**ision is no longer blurred; I know who I am thanks to You.

You are **W**onderful. You are marvelous. Thank You for **W**ashing me and making me clean. Thank You for taking my **W**eaknesses and turning them into strengths. Thank You for **W**orking with me. Thank You for not abandoning me!

Nobody can cross me out by putting an **X** through my name because of You! When folks close one door, You open another. Your **X**-ray eyes can see my heart; You know me and yet You still love me—glory to Your Name forever!

Jesus, **Y**ou are the Holy One! You are the One I **Y**earn for. You are the **Y**oke destroyer. You keep me from being an emotional **Y**o-**Y**o—up one day and down another. Uncertain about my future—NO! I can be steady because of **Y**ou. How can I be so confident—because I'm **Y**ours—I belong to **Y**ou, and **Y**ou are well able to take care of what's **Y**ours.

I **Z**ip through life because of You. I don't walk through life like a **Z**ombie with no hope. I'm alive, I'm alive, I'm alive because of You—thank You, Lord. You are miraculous and *I love You!*

Selah!

Praising From The Valley

By him therefore let us offer the sacrifice of praise to God
continually, that is, the fruit of our lips giving thanks to
his name.

Hebrews 13:15

Most of this book was written *not* when I was on the mountaintop
but when I was in the valley! Even though we tend to focus on
the negatives in our life, praising God will lift us high above any
situation or circumstance.

On payday, we may pay all our bills except two. But we focus
on the two we didn't pay. The next time you find that happening,
praise God for the bills that were paid, and thank Him that the
other two will be.

If you have six kids and all are serving God but two, the enemy
will have you focus on the two who are not. Give a shout of praise
for the four and thank Him that the other two will serve Him as
well. You need to remember that your worst day is a good day in
the life of someone else! There are many people who would trade
lives with you any day.

This next praise was written on Wednesday, August 13, 2003,
at 9:35 p.m. I still had the seventy-two cents in my pocket from
the previous Monday. That summer for me was a rough time. The

Lord instructed me to work for the school system so I could write during the summer, but I would be remiss if I didn't tell you that I was disobedient most of the time. Something always vied for my time, and, sad to say, I yielded to the demands and never did much writing. Because of my disobedience, I didn't prosper, but it was no one's fault but my own. God still provided, even in my disobedience, but I could have been further along financially had I been writing as He instructed me to.

It was near the end of the summer when I finally admitted to God that I was sorry for the days I had secretly pouted. I knew I enjoyed many days of sweet fellowship with the Lord, so I thanked Him that, despite my empty pockets, I was still rich beyond measure. I was healthy, I enjoyed a nice home. I had a great family—not perfect but great. However, I didn't hide the fact that I didn't enjoy not having money in my pocket to indulge in pleasures I had become accustomed to.

I vowed that I was not going to ask anyone for anything anymore. If God didn't do it, I would go without. It was hard. There were many people I could have called on the phone and said, "I have seventy-two cents in my pocket, can you give me twenty dollars?" And they probably would have given me more. But I was determined not to beg (yes, I said *beg*) anyone for money.

That night at church, I ran into several people and my flesh was yelling, "Tell them! Tell them! You're almost out of gas and you have seventy-two cents in your pocket." But I refused to yield.

I listened to the Word, then left church with a smile on my face. Everyone I met asked, "How you doing, girl?" or "Hey, what's going on?" My flesh wanted to say, "I have seventy-two cents in my pocket, and I need some money!" but I didn't. I smiled and said, "Things are great!" and I would leave and go home. Even though I lacked many of the things I desired, I was determined to show a love and appreciation for the Lord that wouldn't even allow me to feel depressed or cry. Praise is not something you do when everything is going great, and you feel like it. Our Heavenly Father is so wonderful and so good to us that even if you only have seventy-two cents, you should not withhold praise. Praise isn't tied to God's pocketbook! Praise is attached to our love for Him and His love for us!

When I got home from church that evening, I really wanted to tune into the Golf Channel. The final PGA Major was going on, and I wanted to see how Tiger Woods was doing. My body didn't want to write, especially about "praise," because I didn't *fe e l* like "praising." But in my heart, I knew I should. I had a mandate from the Lord, and after all, I was only writing what I had been practicing myself, so why should I faint and become weary just because things weren't going well? I was judging my praise by my circumstance and, in reality, my circumstance didn't have anything to do with whether I praised God or not.

Holy Spirit gently reminded me that Tiger Woods—and everyone else on tour —had their millions. It was possible that some of them didn't know or even acknowledge that there was a God. I didn't know, only God knows the heart. I only knew I had an opportunity to praise the Lord, and I was considering choosing Tiger Woods over Him. Determined that my God deserved my obedience, I decided to pen a praise. Sometimes we just need to sit down and think about God's goodness and all that Jesus has done and is doing in our lives, especially during difficult times. Even if you think He's not doing anything, the Bible tells us He's ever interceding for us at the right hand of the Father. (Romans 8:34, KJV, *Who is he that condemneth? It is Christ that died, yea rather, that is risen again, who is even at the right hand of God, who also maketh intercession for us.)* That alone deserves a praise because even in our mess, He's pleading for us something like, "Father, I died for them, we know that better days are ahead, show them your mercy!" Wow, I felt that!

Like me, you may choose to write your praise, but don't stop there. After you write your praise, put down the paper and raise your hands and open your mouth and speak forth the things that come from your heart. Think about where you are right now and how you feel. Emotions will run the gamut. Some of you are very satisfied and happy. Some of you are in a state of euphoria. And some of you feel lonely, depressed, and helpless. No matter what state you are in emotionally, the Lord is with you. He's God when you're on the mountaintop, and He's still God when you're in the valley. You can be alone, but you don't have to be lonely. Things in your life could have regressed, but you don't have to be depressed. Remember, you don't have to feel helpless; you have a Helper.

Read this praise and then I want you to write one based on how you feel at this moment:

> Father, I come to You this evening, thanking You for things in my life that You've done over the years. I refuse to dwell on this moment and all the things I lack. You're so wonderful, I am not going to **A**llow my current situation to dictate that I withhold praise from You. **B**elief in You has **C**arried me. I honor You with my mouth and with my thoughts. **D**etermined to **E**rase all the negatives that I **F**ace, I proclaim my love for You, and I thank You for **G**ently **H**olding me in Your arms.

I can feel Your **I**rresistible pull. **J**udging my surroundings do me no good. But **K**eeping my thoughts on You and **L**oving You despite of what I feel means more to me at this moment than **M**oney in my pocket or any **N**eed I may think I have. If I were honest, the things I long for aren't necessities. There is truly no **O**ne like You. There are no friends I can call who can satisfy me like You. **O**h, to think what life would be without You. My **O**pposition would have a field day! A mess it would be. Just praising You tonight has **P**ropelled me out of my present circumstances. I needed something to get me out of the **Q**uagmire I'm in and **R**ise above it. That something is You. I am **S**ustained by Your love.

Truthfully, I never thought that our relationship would ever get this good, but it has. I now **U**nderstand what my grandmother and saints of old meant when they sang, "What a Friend We Have in Jesus." I refuse to forfeit my peace. No—You paid much too great a price—You paid with Your life. I **V**ow to not let anything come between us. Just You **W**ait and see, I'll love You forever. I've found out by living this thing that love x love = more love. I feel **Y**outhful in Your presence—**Y**oung and in love. **Y**our love times my love equals a life filled with love; how could I lose?

Yes, I sit here and pen from my heart my feelings. No longer am I thinking or concentrating on the things I thought so important an hour ago. I'm just basking in this moment with You. Though the enemy tried to steal my joy—once again my **Z**eal has been exposed. The smile on my face says it all. I'm in love with three very special People, God my Father, Jesus my Lord, and my dearest Friend in the whole wide world...Holy Spirit! You're all so good, so good, yes you are!

No TV program, no phone call from a friend, no flavor of ice cream could have pulled me from where I was over an hour ago to where I am now. I thank You with all my heart—and I am loving You more each day. Your daughter, Gloria!

Folks, I can't begin to tell you how I felt after writing that praise. No money, no man, no friend could bring such joy. As soon as I finished writing, I raised my hands in praise and spoke what I just wrote to the Lord.

Every word of that praise came from my heart. I didn't have to use the dictionary because the flow was there. I believe my overflow came from the reservoir that I've built up. You'll get that way too. There will be times when using the dictionary will be an option, but, as you get proficient in the ABC's of Praise, you'll be so full that you'll just flow. You'll get "lost in His Presence." I most certainly did.

JEHOVAH JIREH—OUR PROVIDER

I will praise thee, O Lord my God, with all my heart:
and I will glorify thy name for evermore.

Psalms 86:12

Life has a way of teaching us that "We're not all that." You begin to realize the only One who is constant with His provision is God. When you've maxed out your credit cards, the 401(k) is gone, and the ATM machine scowls and says, "Don't even try it," you realize that if God does not step in, you're going under.

When you're between a rock and a hard place, give a praise to Jehovah Jireh—your Provider. Come, let us lift up our hands and give Him His due:

> Father, this is an **A**wful situation I'm facing. It seems as though I'm getting **B**eat down on every hand. However, I was reminded today that You're still here. You are and will always be Jehovah Jireh my Provider. My **C**ircumstance has changed, but my **C**ovenant with You still remains. You *will* **D**eliver me out of this situation. I **E**xpect victory because You are **F**aithful. You are **G**od and do not change. You are my very present **H**elp. I am no

longer **I**mmature about Who You are. I know that I can depend on You. So **J**oyfully, I proclaim that I have a **K**een awareness of my past victories and my future in You. I am no longer spiritually dull. I will not **L**ay down and give up because **I** win. Why? Because I have You.

I **M**anage my emotions and I do not **N**eglect my confession of faith. Because I'm **O**bedient and confess what You say about me, **P**ositive things will begin to happen. The enemy can no longer **Q**uell my confidence. I know how to enter into Your **R**est. Thank You, Lord, for being my Provider.

See, You've done it again; **s**uddenly, I no longer feel **T**rapped. I am **U**nmoved by what I see. **V**ague are those things that weighed me down before I entered into Your presence. I can now **W**ait patiently for my deliverance.

Lord, do You realize what effect You have on people? That was really a rhetorical question. I don't expect an answer. I know you know everything!

Being in Your presence one minute can change a life. I know that I can make it! Nobody can talk me out of it! Your love has just covered me with a blanket of peace. Thank You! Thank You! Thank You!

I no longer feel broke down but refreshed. Jesus, You are the **X**O [Executive Officer] in charge of my affairs. I thank **Y**ou that the spirit of heaviness is far from me. No matter how loud the enemy **Y**aks [babble, chatter], my confession of who You are causes him to **Z**ip it up! Satan has to be quiet, because You are the greater One and Holy Spirit lives in me. Yes, I am more than an overcomer! Thank You, Jehovah Jireh, for being my Provider.

Keep Praising—You Have His Ear

Every day will I bless thee; and I will praise thy name for ever and ever.

Psalms 145:2

This particular praise is one to thank God for His ***accessibility***. You don't need to stand in line and take a number; He's always there for you. If you really thought about this statement, it should leave you reeling. Think what would happen if you wanted to talk to the President of the United States. To some, he is the most important person in the world. If you wanted an appointment just to sit down and talk with him—fat chance.

But the God who created the universe; His Son, Jesus, Who gave His life for us; and Holy Spirit, will talk to you at any time. Doesn't that just blow your mind?

I was thinking about this one day and the following praise flowed from my lips. You may not feel this one but write your own. This one will let you know how I feel.

Father, I want to praise and thank You for being **A**ccessible to me. You are so easy to **A**pproach. Your lovingkindness is present even when I miss it. Thank You for helping me to bring **B**alance into my life, that mental stability I need. The Confidence I have in You will never Cease to exist, because there is no end to You. I thank You for my grandparents, and parents, who never Debated Your existence. They never quarreled or questioned You, which allowed me to grow up knowing You did Exist indeed! I thank You that I've always been Free to call on the Name of the Lord. Until today, I never really realized the wonderful Gift my parents instilled in me as a Girl—that You were a real Person to be respected and Honored. While I've always paid Homage to You, for many years, I was Ignorant of Who You were, and how much Your Son Jesus had to pay for me. As a little girl, I watched grown-ups throw their hands in the air to praise You; I thought they were Kooks—eccentric, strange people. But now I realize they had something more precious than I could even imagine. Love makes you strange to those who haven't yet experienced love—especially being in Love with You.

You're Majestic; a royal, Magnificent God who brightens the heart and lifts the heads of those whose countenance has been darkened by the things of the world. Never could I ever foresee how much You would mean to me and be a part of my life. My Objective is to infect as many people as possible with Your wonderful love. Personally, I'm surprised myself at the effect You have on me. I refuse to Quarrel with individuals while trying to defend Your existence. Why get involved in an angry dispute with ill-informed people?

The facts all point to You. Life has a way of **R**emoving the **S**cales that blind unbelief. **S**ooner or later **T**ruth prevails, and they will have an **U**rgency to **U**nderstand why those who love and cherish You feel like we do. **U**ntil then—their hearts will be **V**acant, empty, **V**oid of the love that can only be filled by **Y**ou.

What a **W**aste to live life without You. It's impossible to be **W**hole unless You're an intricate part of one's life.

I'm just so thankful that each day I wake up You're mine and I don't have to share my time alone with You with anyone! **Y**ielding to You was the smartest decision I've ever made. You're **X**-tra large in my life and You belong to me! Thank You for the constant **Z**est in our relationship. I enjoy and love You with all my heart!

See, you have to think about this kind of praise, it doesn't just roll off your lips. You must spend some time – but it's worth it!

Let Nothing Block You From Loving God

The Lord is my strength and my shield; my heart trusted in him, and I am helped: therefore my heart greatly rejoiceth; and with my song will I praise him.

Psalms 28:7

Once you develop a relationship with God, you will become increasingly more conscious of His goodness and character. Your heart will become even more tender. You'll find yourself holding your hands up as you go through the house saying, "Lord, thank You; Father, I just love You so much!" And when you love someone, it's e-a-s-y to give praise. Conversely, if you're angry or mad, it's difficult.

I have three children and eight grandchildren. I constantly shower praises on them. When they're in my presence, praise rolls off my tongue because of our relationship. When I'm angry with them, and yes, there are times when the relationship is challenged, there is not much praise coming from my lips.

Between the ages of approximately sixteen and thirty, when I was a babe in the Lord, I didn't give praise. I was not taught to praise Him, and frankly, I had some issues with God that kept me from praising Him.

My mom died when she was fifty-seven, and I was still very young in the Lord. I loved my mom very much. She was sweet, easygoing, and very lovable. While I never verbalized my feelings to God, I blamed Him for letting her die. After all, He was God, He could do anything; why didn't He save my mom? Well, little did I know at the time that the person to blame was not God. If we read our Bible -- and back then I was reading everything but my Bible-- God gives us some clear directions on how we treat our "temples/bodies.". We have only one body, and if we abuse it, it will give out on us.

God also tells us to pray for one another. Once I began to read the Bible for myself, I realized that my mother played a part in leaving early, and I, as her daughter, didn't do my part either. Yes, I was ignorant of prayer and how to pray, but ignorance is no excuse, and it has its price. When I saw behavior contrary to the Word of God in my mother's life, I didn't pray. When my mom was in the hospital, my prayers weren't faith filled or laced with the Word. I had not been taught. That's why I encourage anyone reading this book to get in a church where the Word is taught. There you will learn about your authority as a believer. I feel I could have done something to help if I had only known better—but I didn't.

I was never taught how to pray, even though I attended church almost every Sunday from the time I was a little girl. The churches I attended had the grown-ups pray, and even when I was in my twenties, the deacon's prayed. In all the churches I attended before I went to Word of Faith, someone else prayed. Don't misunderstand me...my Grandmother who was a Pastor led me to Christ and taught me to love and honor God; which I'm eternally grateful for. But back then not much Bible was taught. When I started going to Word of Faith and subsequently joined, it was there that I was taught to pray according to the Word. And it was there where I was also taught to **read** my Bible. It was there that I learned how to have an intimate relationship with God.

Fast forward years later, my dad, who I loved with all my heart, came to live with me when he was about sixty-four years old. At the time, he was an alcoholic, and I didn't drink. I must be honest and tell you that I did not want my father to come live with me for that reason alone. And I thought it would be the excuse that would release me from having him come live with me. But Holy Spirit knows how to get your attention in such a Gentlemanly way. While I was focusing on my dad's drinking, Holy Spirit reminded me that I was a chocoholic (chocolate lover) and chickaholic (fried chicken lover) and, at the time, I didn't have control over either. My chocolate called me like my dad's alcohol called him. Whereas my dad drank in abundance the first of the month after receiving his check, I cooked fried chicken in abundance every week I got paid. When I began to look at myself and all the things I needed to control, I no longer judged my dad.

As Christians, we sometimes forget our struggles, and we focus too much on what we perceive is sin in others. The Word says in Matthew 7:3–5: *"And why beholdest thou the mote that is in thy brother's eye, but considerest not the beam that is in thine own eye? Or how wilt thou say to thy brother, Let me pull out the mote out of thine eye; and behold, a beam is in thine own eye? Thou Hypocrite, first cast out the beam out of thine own eye; and then shalt thou see clearly to cast out the mote out of thy brother's eye."* When God tells you to do something, don't try to wiggle out of it by telling Him what another person is doing wrong. He didn't ask me for excuses. He gave me a directive, and my approach to wanting Dad delivered from alcoholism should have been different. My love should have been the driving force instead of judgment. It was easy for me to see Dad's sins, because I had taken my eyes off mine. God wanted my dad delivered, but He wanted me delivered as well.

God does not want us to become experts at judging others. Instead, He wants us to be diligent at judging ourselves. Matthew 7:1–2 reads: *"Judge not, that ye be not judged. For with what judgment ye judge, ye shall be judged: and with what measure ye mete, it shall be measured to you again."* I was looking for excuses, but God dealt with my heart, and I'm so glad He did.

Because my dad came to live with me, *after* I received years of "teaching," and "Bible reading," and a heart that was changed, my prayers for him were Word based and effective. Unlike the prayers I had prayed for my mom, I'm not judging anyone; I'm mainly sharing my story.

My kids and I would lay hands on my dad and pray for him. Our prayers, along with those of my brothers and sisters and others, made a difference. Because of spiritual growth—history did not repeat itself.

Even before my dad moved in with me, I constantly covered him with prayer, something I didn't do for my mom . . . I prayed that even in his foolishness (drinking until he passed out), that the angels of the Lord would protect him and keep him from danger. I prayed that people would not take advantage of him while he was in a drunken stupor. I prayed that God would preserve him.

A week before my dad came to live with me, I told him, "Dad, you know I don't drink, and I don't allow drinking in my home. If you come to live with me, you must promise that you won't drink." My Dad's reply, "Baby, I will quit—Daddy won't drink."

Now, under normal circumstances, I wouldn't have even thought about believing him, because he had promised many,

many times before that he was going to quit, only to take another drink. The difference in his promise to me, however, was the fact that I had prayed for deliverance, and I knew by then that God not only hears but He answers as well. I believed that He would answer my prayer.

Dad lived with me for seven years until he went to be with the Lord at seventy-two, and he never drank in my house. I can count a few times early on in that seven-year stretch when some of his friends picked him up and brought him back drunk; however, after my brief and candid conversation with them—when I in no uncertain terms told them to "never let that happen again"—I didn't have to deal with the alcohol anymore.

What was the difference in my mom and dad? Prayer. There were other issues, but the lack of prayer on my part was one. You may say, "And what does this have to do with praise?" During my mother's illness and a couple of years after her death, I came to grips with the truth that God wasn't responsible.

I could not praise God even if I knew how back then, because I blamed Him for my mom's death. How can you praise someone who let your mom die? How could I tell God how wonderful He is when I thought He was responsible for my mom's death? How can you lift your hands and proclaim that a Person is the greatest when you think He turned His back on you during one of the most critical times in your life?

If you're harboring negative feelings about God, you won't praise Him. If you're mad at God and you believe He's part of the problem and not the solution—you won't praise Him. But I've come to set you free, if you want freedom. God didn't do it! No matter what someone told you, or no matter if all evidence points toward Him, trust me, He is innocent and He didn't cause your sorrow.

John 10:10–11, KJV says, *"The thief cometh not, but for to steal, and to kill, and to destroy: I am come that they might have life, and that they might have it more abundantly. I am the good shepherd: the good shepherd giveth his life for the sheep."*

We do have a real enemy, but it is not God. Why would Someone give His Son so we could be saved, if He was the bad guy? Why would Jesus die on the cross if His Father wanted to "make us pay?" Why would Jesus give us Holy Spirit to lead, guide, and direct us if God wanted to "get us?"

You need to get over being angry with God. Get rid of any blame so that you can boldly raise your hands in praise to the God who so deserves it! If you're withholding your praise because you blame God for something—repent (1 John 1:9). Tell God you're sorry and pray Luke 12:2. Ask God to reveal to you what happened to cause your anger, then believe and request that God send someone across your path who will help you find answers. Then begin to read your Bible.

I prayed the following prayer for all of you who might harbor anger in your hearts as I wrote this book. Read this prayer and open your heart to receive a breakthrough.

> Dear Heavenly Father, I come to You on behalf of the person reading this book who may have an issue of the heart. They need Divine intervention on Your behalf. Provide answers, wisdom, revelation, and healing as only You can. Father, send laborers across their paths that will help them to see how wonderful You are and people who will help them find answers to the concerns they have. Father, help them find a church that

will provide godly counsel from the Word of God. Grow them up spiritually so that once they're delivered, they will help others who are in need. Thank You, Father, that those who once hurt, hurt no more. Thank You for healing them and setting them free in the Name of Jesus I pray—Amen.

I know God answers my prayers and He will answer yours. Receive your deliverance and, as an act of your faith, thank God now for the load that has been lifted from your shoulders.

Now that you're free, never pass up an opportunity to praise. When you feel it, say it! When you don't feel like it, say it! I don't care where you are or how "silly" you may feel. Only the devil will try to make you feel ridiculous when it comes to praise. But trust me—God is smiling and that's all that counts. If you're at a formal dinner, I'm not telling you to jump up with your tuxedo on and holler, "Glory to God!" Just look up while everyone else is talking about their achievements and say under your breath, "God even at this boring formal dinner, I see and feel Your love, and I just want to thank You."

As you lie in bed tonight, instead of saying your regular prayer, try mixing your prayer with praise using the *ABC's of Praise*. You can do half of the alphabet tonight and think of the other half for tomorrow. Perhaps it will go something like this...

> Father, as I lie here in the bed You've blessed me with, I just want to tell You how grateful I am to You for all You've done.
>
> Despite of my day, You've seen to it that I'm **A**lert, **B**athed, and **C**omfortable in a bed that

You've provided for me. As I listened to the news and saw that **D**anger was all around, none came nigh my dwelling.

I lie here **E**xcited at Your Word in Psalms 4:8 that says, *"I will both lay me down in peace, and sleep: for thou, Lord, only makest me dwell in safety."* That tells me You knew that I'd be living in this neighborhood a long time ago, and You still said I would "dwell in safety." You also said in Proverbs 3:24 that, *"When thou liest down, thou shalt not be afraid: yea, thou shalt lie down, and thy sleep shall be sweet."* So, I will not be **F**earful. Thank You, Father, for Your protection and sweet sleep.

You've blessed me with **F**ood to eat, I'm **G**ifted with Your presence. As I lay down tonight and when I awake in the morning, my Friend, precious **H**oly Spirit, will be here with me. If I face anything, **H**elp is not on the way, **Help** is **H**ere with me. You're my **I**ncentive for getting out of bed tomorrow. I also thank You for helping me **J**uggle the many assignments I had today. It was You who caused me to have victory. Thank You, Lord, for my **K**infolk, continue to save those who are in need of You. I give You praise for Your protection over them today and ask for continued blessings on tomorrow. Bless them with the desires that line-up with Your Word. May they, too, lift holy hands to praise You.

When I get up in the morning, I'll honor You by walking in **L**ove, and last but not least—may

I never forget how magnificent You are, in Jesus's Name—Amen.

Now isn't that better than "Now I lay me down to sleep?"

Praise When You're Naughty

I will call upon the Lord, who is worthy to be praised: so shall I be saved from mine enemies.

Psalms 18:3

We must recognize that God deserves praise in every situation.

There are several definitions of praise, one being "the expression of gratitude for personal favors conferred." Praise can't get any more personal than when we *know* we've done something real dumb and *didn't* get what we deserved.

Let's not forget that when we praise God, we are telling Him thanks for the many things He has done for us. Praising Him, especially in difficult circumstances, helps us forget our problems and realize that we have a Friend who is always willing to comfort us. That's why I wanted to show you how we can praise God for the "naughty" things we've done, the stupid moves we've made, and the danger from which He rescued us. If we were out in the world and someone rescued us, we would thank them or bestow accolades upon them. Then why not do that much more for God? He deserves our praise, too.

Come to know God for being in the middle of everything you do. And praise Him for everything. Consider this scenario: You've had a bad day and did not act or respond to some situation as you should have—you've been naughty instead of nice. When that happens, you can do one of two things: You can beat yourself up, or you can slip over into praise. The benefit of the *ABC's of Praise* is that you must force your mind to get in sync with your spirit. Make yourself start with a word that begins with *A* and go all the way to *Z*, thinking about how God intervened and how you're going to give Him praise.

First, recall the situation. Raise your hands when you think about what *could* have happened. Then start your praise . . .

Absolutely, Father, I am Ashamed of the way I Acted today. But as always, You Brought me out of my Crisis. My Circle of so-called friends Couldn't even restrain me. You, however, Delivered me before I could Destroy my testimony. Did I Deserve the mercy? No. Did I Deserve the grace? No. But You saw fit to once again Extend to me Your kindness. I see clearly now what happens when we are Eager to take matters into our own hands instead of doing things Your way.

The Enemy set a perfect trap for me today. Eyes wide open, I Fell into it. No, it was not Your Fault, because Your Word has taught me over and over to Forgive. But I chose this day to *react.* I let my Guard down, Gave into the pressure. But You Holy Spirit helped me Gather my thoughts so that I could get a Handle on the situation. Oh, the Hazard of yielding to the flesh. I stand before You now, Honoring You. I can't Ignore Your power when I yield to it. God, Imagine what would have happened if I had continued to Ignore Holy

Spirit. The **I**mage of what could have happened is frightening, to say the least. My faith and all that I represent would have been the **J**oke of the office. I was in **J**eopardy of losing my testimony.

I **K**neel before You, Lord. You deserve all the **K**udos. Thank You once again for saving me from myself. What **L**essons I have **L**earned . . . **L**eave situations when you know they are escalating. **L**abor to do the right thing. The **L**ack of Your Word is detrimental to my **L**egacy in You. **L**ord, my **M**ission is to please You, I've made **M**any **M**istakes before; today was no exception. But thanks to You my spiritual **M**uscles are becoming well developed, becoming defined in the things of God, and **M**aturing, thanks to Holy Spirit.

Nay, I am more than a conqueror, because I've come to know that I **N**eed this time with You to express my appreciation. To some, I'm just a **N**umber, but to You, I'm a daughter who is cherished and loved. **N**ever have I **N**eeded You more than **N**ow to **N**urse the wounds that life inflicts on us all. Your sweet **O**il of gladness is so soothing. It just pays to **O**bey You. Thank You for being my **O**asis, thank You for taking away the **P**ain.

How can I **P**ay You for all You've done? You're the only **P**erson I know who forgives and forgets, once I confess my sin to You. I can bring anything to You. You've never told me my issues were too **P**etty. You never **P**ick and choose the sins You'll forgive. When I come to You asking for forgiveness, You forgive all. I'm so thankful.

You are **Q**uite something! Simply remarkable! My constant **R**efuge, my **R**elief and **R**eason for existing. **R**efresh me, Holy Spirit. **S**trengthen me, **S**ustain me where I'm weak—I *can* be **S**trong because of You. Continue to **T**each, **T**rain, and **T**ake me to levels I never knew I could reach. **U**ncover areas in my life that are **U**nholy and **U**nhealthy; areas I can change with the help of Holy Spirit.

With Your help, **V**ictory belongs to me. With Your help I can be a **Virtuous** person. With Your help, nothing is **V**oid in my life.

Thank You for **W**ashing me in Your Blood. Thank You, Jesus, for **W**inning the **W**ar. Thank You for Your **W**onderful presence, Holy Spirit. You are large, no, You're better than large, You're **X**-tra large in my life. I **Y**earn to be more like **Y**ou, Jesus, and in my **Y**earning, sometimes I just have to **Y**awl [cry out] because of **Y**our patience with me. **Y**ea, Your company is sweet. I'll be passionate in my pursuit of **Y**our Word. May my **Z**eal never wane [it won't diminish, decrease, or decline]. Like **Z**eri in 1 Chronicles 25:3, I shall continue to *praise You at all times*, even when I act *stupid!*

When you do this, you've embraced God's love even in the difficult times. As a result, you won't continue to beat yourself up.

You move on quicker, and you've become vulnerable to the One Who loves you more than anyone else in the world!

It took me some time to write this praise because I had to think about this scenario and get the dictionary. You might need to do the same. But you will have spent quality time praising God.

Often, we are so lazy. We are satisfied using the same words and expressions over and over, but God wants us to branch out. He wants us to increase our vocabulary when we talk to Him. When we do that, we will be able to better express to Him how we feel. As you build your vocabulary praising God, you'll express yourself better in your everyday life!

Can't you see the Father's face when you admit, "God You're too big, I'm at a loss for what I want to say. But telling You how I feel is really important to me right now, so bear with me, Father, I'm going to the dictionary. I'm going to dig and search and look until I find the words to express to You, Who You are and how I feel about You right now, because You mean that much to me!"

Our Heavenly Father and Jesus are looking at you with Their chest sticking out because They're thinking, "They could have given up and turned on the TV, but it means that much to them, that they are willing to go to the dictionary to express their love to Us! What, you say!"

Others In The Bible Who Praised

Bless the Lord, O my soul: and all that is within me, bless his holy name.

Psalms 103:1

There are many examples in the Bible of people who offered up praise to God, and their praise wasn't limited to the times when everything was going well for them.

Leah was the first wife of Jacob, not by choice, but by default. Her story is told in Genesis, Chapters 29 to 35. Leah was a woman who, through trickery, found herself married to a man who was more in love with her sister Rachel. Leah lived her life in the shadow of her younger sister, competing for her husband's love. She even thought that by having Jacob's children she would win the love she wanted so badly. It didn't work then, and it won't work now.

Four boys later, Leah finally saw the light. She named her fourth son Judah, and, instead of thinking about her husband, she thought about God and realized God loved her. He had seen her tears and had shown her favor by opening her womb and blessing her with children. In Genesis 29:35 she forgot about her husband and herself and said, "Now will I praise the Lord." Later she bore more children, but she never won the place in her husband's heart for which she yearned.

Many of us look for love in all the wrong places. The world would make us feel unloved and unappreciated, but God loved us so much that He gave His only Son, proving His love for us. While others reject us, God has always and will always love us. We should always direct our energy and bless the Lord with our praise. Praise Him for His love.

Has God blessed you with children? Praise Him for your children. They may not be everything you want them to be, but we haven't been perfect parents either; and remember, your child's story is still being written.

If you begin to praise God for your children, you'll see things change. It's a blessing from God to have an open, fertile womb. Don't even think it's because you're all that, it's because God has blessed you and He deserves praise.

If you haven't had children yet and you and your husband desire them, pray for your womb to open in the Name of Jesus and start giving God praise for your children, and watch that womb open up. Speak faith daily and then send me a praise report later.

Deborah was a military leader, prophet, judge, and wife. Her story is told in Judges, Chapters 4 and 5. Deborah was in leadership when it was unusual for a woman to be in a position of authority. Her example shows you that when God appoints you, it doesn't matter what the norm may be at that particular time—no one will be able to stop your promotion.

After winning a great battle, instead of touting what a great military leader she was, Deborah chose to sing praises to God. It would have been very easy for her to credit her smarts and wisdom, reminding the people, "It took a woman to do this!" But Deborah was smarter than that. She gave credit to the One who deserved it. Deborah and Barak sang praises in Chapter 5, verse 2 of Judges.

What victories or accomplishments have you patted yourself on the back for, neglecting to praise God? Has God won any battles for you lately? Has He gotten you out of any messes? Has He avenged you like he avenged Israel? Like Deborah and Barak, give God some praise. Now would be a good time to lift your hands and thank Him.

Deborah also served as a judge who settled disputes. Has God been your judge and settled some legal affairs and personal arguments? Lift those hands again and praise Him.

David was a shepherd boy, warrior, and king. His story begins in 1 Samuel, Chapter 16 through 1 Kings 2, and is told throughout the Bible ending in Hebrews 11:32 a Chapter known as the Faith Hall of Fame. David, as we know, was a great king who had some great mess ups as well. However, he loved God. At the end of his life, David wanted to rebuild the temple for God, but God told him through the prophet Nathan (2 Samuel 7:1–13 and 1 Kings 8:17–19) that his seed (Solomon) would build the temple. David didn't get mad at God. Instead, he made sure that his son was successful in this endeavor. He began to put in place strategies to ensure the success of the temple's construction.

David's story continues in 1 Chronicles 23:1–30. He gathered all Israel's leaders, men at least thirty years of age, and gave them assignments. In the midst of assigning officials, judges, and supervisors, David assigned four thousand men to praise the Lord by playing musical instruments David had given them. But he didn't stop there. Whenever he made assignments for specific duties, David also called this group to give thanks and praise to God every morning and evening. Wow! Some leaders would view this as a waste of manpower—not David. He constantly reminded those he ruled that God's ever-present help in their lives deserved praise. I believe that's just one of the reasons for David's success. Psalms, which is divided into Divisions, is also filled with praises from David.

Are you a leader who emphasizes praise to God for what He's done in your life? Amidst the everyday finagling to get the job done, does God get the praise He deserves for your success? If you were moved from your position tomorrow, would people know that praise was a part of your legacy? Perhaps you don't have the manpower or authority to assign praisers, but you can be one. I know that many of you are already, but what about the rest of you? Give God praise for your company.

Paul and Silas sang loud praises while in jail (Acts 16:25). Do you think in the natural they felt like praising? Most of us would have been having a conversation that would go something like this. . . "Man, see what we get for obeying God. We should have shut up and got out of here." They didn't focus on the 'why' they were in jail. Their thoughts were on the Who they served. No, they probably didn't feel like praising, but they did it anyway and what happened? God sent an earthquake and released them from jail.

Zacharias was struck dumb for months, yet when his tongue was loosed, and he could finally talk, his first words were praises to Almighty God (Luke 1:64). Think about that for a moment. His baby was eight days old when his tongue was loosed. Most people's first words would be, "Give me my son!" Not Zacharias, he praised God!

Look up others in the Bible who were in difficult situations but chose to praise rather than pout. Be one of them.

The Book Of Praise: Psalms

For the Lord is great, and greatly to be praised: he is to be feared above all gods.

Psalms 96:4

The book of Psalms is filled with praise. Within each Division there are stanzas where you should spend some time and allow God's Spirit to minister to you about praise. It takes approximately four hours (give or take depending on you) to read the entire book of Psalms, not meditate on them, but only to read them. What a perfect way to spend an evening or weekend afternoon!

While you're reading Psalms, circle, star, or highlight Scripture that talks about praise. Then commit some of the Scriptures to memory, so you can confess them out of your mouth.

Let me just share an example from my own life of why praise is so important. While working in a suburban high school, I noticed that when students came into the office, more often than not, they were rude, obnoxious, and noisy. Their attitude demanded that you stopped what you were doing *NOW* to solve their problems, which were critical to them. Each child acted as if they were the only kid in school.

Children behave that way. Most of them are only concerned with their issues and, the majority of the time, their issues are not issues at all. But to these kids they were mountains that needed to be moved ASAP. If we gently corrected their attitude or approach, some stormed out of Student Services, mumbling and yelling expletives. This went on day after day. Believe it or not, many of the parents acted the same way.

Then, once in a blue moon, there were those kids who would come in and say, "Hi Ms. Pruett. I just came in to see you and tell you to have a good day." I wanted to jump over the counter and hug them. Of course, I couldn't, but just hearing a friendly voice bearing glad tidings was like a breath of fresh air. When students did this, I would find a way to bless them.

As I thought about these students, Holy Spirit said to me, "How do you think God feels? Everyday, millions of His children, from different backgrounds, come into His presence. Some are rude, others sulk, and their attitude demands that God fix their problems *NOW*, which they deemed critical. Some, like the high school kids, don't even say 'hello' to God. They just spout off their concerns and issues, not even thinking once about God and His feelings."

Imagine people worldwide asking, begging, blaming, crying, and speaking unbelief. Can you envision how our Father feels with Jesus next to Him SHH (Shaking His Head) I made this up.

Now picture with me how They feel when we come to Them and say, "God, how was Your day? Jesus, have I told You lately how much I adore You? Do You realize You are the reason I choose to live right?" How many of you just come into Their presence stretching your arms out saying how blessed you are to have a Dad like Him and a Savior like Jesus!

If God can get jealous, and Jesus can cry, they can also hurt when we fail to offer due praise. We need to continually honor

God. Let me give you Scripture for what I just said. In Exodus 20:5; 34:14; Deuteronomy 4:24; 5:9; 6:15; Joshua 24:19; and Nahum 1:2 Scripture refers to God being jealous of anything that's put before Him. One verse even says that His Name is "Jealous." John 11:35 says, "Jesus wept." Here Jesus was in the midst of friends who were hurting and weeping because Lazarus had died. Seeing all the pain, Jesus wept as well. If He didn't have feelings, He wouldn't have cried.

When we act like we care about God and we're not ashamed to show Him love and affection, there is nothing God won't do for us. Promise yourself to be God's child who will give Him glory and honor. Let God know that you appreciate Him. When He hears your voice, it should be music to His ears. His chest should swell as He says, "Listen to My child—his/her words are like music to My ears." Remember the Scripture in 1 Corinthians 2:9: *"But as it is written, Eye hath not seen, nor ear heard, neither have entered into the heart of man, the things which God hath prepared for them that love him."*

God and Jesus have proven Their faithfulness to us over and over again. Let's be faithful in our praise to Them. It doesn't cost anything but, the yielding of our tongue, and a grateful heart.

One Labor Day, my children (who are all grown) were not around. I was by myself—but not alone. I decided the day before to cook outside so that I could have a quiet day to write I am beginning to see that it is not only a gift, but a passion. I got up praising God, but not with my usual *ABC's*. Instead, I decided to be Spirit led.

I proceeded to tidy up, prepare my clothes for the week and wash clothes, all the while focusing on and giving thanks to the Lord. I put on a Christian video (teaching tape) while folding clothes and gave praises as the minister poured out truths from God's Word that were truths in my life as well.

Then it was time to wash, press, and curl my hair (that's a praise report in and of itself). I turned off the video and put on a CD. As the lyrics bellowed praises, I found myself putting down the straightening comb and curlers, making a decision that praise was more important. I could do my hair later.

When my mind began to wander, I did what the Word said and quoted God's promises. Sometime during that day, I said my *ABC's of Praise*. The devil kept trying to bring ugly thoughts to me, but I quoted Scripture from my friend David in the Bible, which said, *"Thy words have I hid in my heart that I might not sin against you."* Those ugly thoughts left as fast as they tried to come.

Sometimes when you are alone, the enemy will try to fill your mind with thoughts that are ungodly, but praise acts like a shield that will help you keep the darts from connecting.

When I completed my to-do list, it was 6:00 p.m. I sat down to write. Before typing a word, however, I was acutely aware of a wonderful peace. I felt like a person who didn't have a care in the world. I reflected that I had been smiling all day, enjoying the company of Someone I love dearly.

When you find yourself alone, turn off the TV. Don't look for the phone to call someone. Take the opportunity to praise all day. Having a day of thanking God and praising Him is sweet.

Maybe you'll choose to go through the Bible and find scriptures on praise or just sit and read the book of Psalms. Maybe like me, you'll just want to praise out of your overflow. Continued praise will take you places you've never been before.

Each section of this book begins with Scripture that talks about praise. Here are a few more references for you from Psalms: Psalms

9:2, 11, 14; 18:49; 21:13; 22:3, 22, 23; 34:1; 35:28; 44:8; 45:17; 47:6; 48:1; 50:23; 56:4; 57:7; 66:8; 67:3; 68:32; 69:30, 34; 71:6, 14; 74:21; 75:9; 79:13; 92:1; 96:2, 4; 98:4; 102:18; 106:1, 48; 107:8 (This exact stanza is repeated several more times, 107:15, 21, and 31); 108:1, 3; 109:1, 30; 111:1; 112:1; 113:1, 3, 9; 115:12, 18; 116:19; 118:19, 21; 119:7, 164, 171, 175; 134:1; 135:1, 21; 138:1; 139:14; 144:9; 145:4, 10, 21; 146:1; 147:7, 12; 148:1–5, 7, 13; 149:1, 3, 6; 150:1–5. Read them, highlight them, and commit some to memory, you'll be glad you did! ☺

Don't Quit -- Keep Praising!

> *Praise ye the Lord: for it is good to sing praises unto our God; for it is pleasant; and praise is comely.*

> Psalms 147:1

I'm going to challenge you to never quit growing in your praise toward God. Perhaps one day, you'll write a book to help people go even higher. I want you to use this section to write two more praises. Use doubles or triples. Write a song or a poem but write two praises. It may take you a couple of days, but you can do it. Listen to Holy Spirit because He knows what's in your heart, and He'll help you write it.

Do you remember the twenty-six things I wrote to help you achieve your desire to "raise your praise and get lost in Him?" Refer back to that section and re-read the confession. You'll be encouraged.

Praise 1: Wrsite your words first.

A= _____

B= _____

C= _____

D= _____

E= _____

F= _____

G= _____

H= _____

I= _____

J= _____

K= _____

L= _____

M= _____

N= _____

O= _____

P= _____

Q= _____

R= _____

S= _____

T= _____

U= _____

V= _____

W= _____

X= _____

Y= _____

Z= _____

Now pen your praise from the words you've written:

_____

_____

_____

_____

_____

_____

_____

_____

_____

_____

_____

_____

_____

_____

Praise 2: Write your words first.

A= _____

B= _____

C= _____

D= _____

E= _____

F= _____

G= _____

H= _____

I= _____

J= _____

K= _____

L= _____

M= _____

N= _____

O= _____

P= _____

Q= _____

R= _____

S= _____

T= _____

U= _____

V= _____

W= _____

X= _____

Y= _____

Z= _____

Now pen your praise from the words you've written:

_____

_____

_____

_____

_____

_____

_____

_____

_____

_____

_____

_____

_____

_____

I'm sure if your experience is anything like mine, you're grinning from ear to ear.

USE SCRIPTURE AS YOUR *ABC's OF PRAISE*

Thou art my God, and I will praise thee: thou art my God, I will exalt thee.

Psalms 118:28

This particular praise is written using Scripture. I really like this one because it's God's Word.

Father, thank You for Your **A**ngels You've given charge over me, so that I won't even dash my foot against a stone. Psalms 91:11

Lord, I will **B**less You today and every day. Praises of You will continually flow from my mouth. Psalms 34:1

Jesus, You died for me so that I could **C**lobber the enemy. I am more than a **C**onqueror through You! Thanks for all You've done. Romans 8:37

Father, I am **D**elivered from the power of darkness because of Your Dear Son, and I'm grateful. Colossians 1:13

Father, I thank You for giving me **E**ternal life through Your Son Jesus. John 3:15

Thank You, Father, for not showing **F**avoritism. You love me as much as You love anyone else, that's because you have no respect of persons. Romans 2:11

Lord, You are **G**reat and **G**reatly to be praised. Psalms 48:1

I thank You, Lord, that I don't have to fear men because You are my **H**elper. Who can come against me and win? Nobody! I will not be scared!! Hebrews 13:6

God, You made me in Your **I**mage—a copy of You. I know some good people, but there is no one on earth I'd rather be a replica of other than You. Oh, how I worship You! Genesis 1:27

Father, You are not just my **J**oy but You're my exceeding **J**oy. Your **J**oy is above and beyond anything I can imagine. When the world says I should be sad, that exceeding **J**oy kicks in. When all is not going well, that exceeding **J**oy bubbles up in my soul. Thank You for Your **J**oy that's greater than anything I could imagine. Psalms 43:4

Jesus, You are such the Gentleman. You stand at the door and **K**nock when You could have flexed Your finger or kicked the door in. Thank You for not leaving and allowing me to come to my senses and open the door to You, and all that You give. You have never forced anything on me. That's another reason why I love You so much. Revelation 3:20

You promised me that no one could come between our **L**ove, nothing—never. I can't be separated from You, not by distress, persecution, famine or even death! You are truly an awesome God. Romans 8:35

Father, great and **M**arvelous are Thy works, great and **M**arvelous are Thy works! Revelation 15:3

Jesus Your Name alone makes the devil tremble and You have given me the authority to use that Name and ask You anything— what a privilege, what an honor. Thank You for trusting me with such a precious **N**ame. John 16:23

I am a world **O**vercomer, and I got that way by believing that Jesus is the Son of God, what perks. Thank You, Lord! 1 John 5:5

You are my hiding place who **P**reserves, who keeps me from trouble, what a caring God You are. Psalms 32:7

God, thank You for Your **Q**uick Word that's alive and full of power. Because Your Word is **Q**uick—and alive—I speak Your Word and things happen! Hebrews 4:12

Lord, You are my **R**edeemer who keeps me from destruction; nobody and nothing can do that but You, and I honor You! Psalms 103:4

Lord, You are the **S**atisfier who fills my mouth with good things. Thank You! Psalms 103:5

Lord, You are the great **T**ransformer who turns me into Your likeness. 2 Corinthians 3:18

Jesus, Thank You for dying for the **U**ngodly—that was me before I accepted You. Romans 5:6

Jesus, because I'm Your sheep, I know Your **V**oice and I hear You—You are not obscure to me. I will follow You, and as I follow Your **V**oice—no one can pluck me out of Your hands. I will flee from the stranger's voice, and I will not follow him. I love You, my Shepherd. John 10: 4–5, 27–28

Jesus, because I'm Your **W**orkmanship, I don't have to feel inferior to anyone. Thank You for my self-esteem that cannot be taken away. Ephesians 2:10

God, "**X**" represents multiplication and You've promised in Your Word to multiply my seeds that I sow, so that I can increase. You could have just "added" my seeds, but no, You're the God of too much, You've got multiplication on Your mind and I am so honored and grateful for what You do for me. 2 Corinthians 9:10

Because of You, Lord my **Y**outh is renewed as the eagle—what love! Psalms 103:5

Thank You, Lord, I am **Z**ealous of Your laws because they keep me out of trouble. Acts 21:20

It's time for another praise exercise. I want you to research Scripture and use the following pages to write your praise. It may take a while to complete the praise because you will start with the letter *A* and go to *Z*. When you finish, lift your hands, and voice your praise. Remember, find the Scripture, write the praise in a sentence, and don't forget to record the Scripture reference.

Begin to write your Scripture praise:

_____

_____

_____

_____

_____

_____

_____

_____

_____

_____

_____

_____

_____

Praise Filled With Thanksgiving

Offer unto God thanksgiving; and pay thy vows unto the most High: And call upon me in the day of trouble: I will deliver thee, and thou shalt glorify me.

Psalms 50:14-15

There are many reasons why we give thanks, but we often forget to be thankful for some of the things we take for granted.

You need to be careful when you allow yourself to slip into that "woe is me" funk. The Bible has something to say about people who are not thankful. For example, Romans 1:21–22 says: *"Because that, when they knew God, they glorified him not as God, neither were thankful; but became vain in their imaginations, and their foolish heart was darkened. Professing themselves to be wise, they became foolish."*

You are a foolish person when you become thankless—when you begin to say, "What do I have to be thankful for?" Read the following praise, then read it again substituting your own words.

Nothing I can do or say will cause You to **A**bandon me! Wow! You're so faithful.

I thank You, Lord, for **B**elieving in me and allowing me the opportunity to enjoy life.

I thank You for Cradling me in Your arms when I needed Your Comfort. You're Consistent with Your love.

Father, thank You for the Detailed way in which You created each one of us. We were so important to You that no one person has the same fingerprint out of the billions of people on earth. Even our teeth are unique. You didn't compare, or copy us, You chose to create originals, because our worth meant that much to You. When You made one, You threw away the mold.

You blessed us with various Emotions that only You could have given and placed within us. You allowed us to feel the wonderfulness of love. We can share laughter. We know that we can overcome hurts and disappointments. Yes, even when we fail, we experience the anticipation and excitement of trying again. Why? Because we know we will experience the thrill of victory!

Thank You for allowing us to Feel the warmth of a hug. The passion of a kiss. A father's and a mother's love. Not to mention the excitement at the birth of a child and to witness that child's innocence.

Father, thank You for putting a little extra something in Grandchildren. What joy we receive just looking at them. You didn't have to do that, but You did.

We have Hope because of You. We have Holy Spirit to Help guide, counsel and encourage us through life. We have Houses to protect us from the elements.

Thank You for not judging us on our Ignorance, blaming You for disasters and personal calamities. You told us in John 10:10 that it is the enemy who comes to steal, kill, and destroy.

Jesus, You came so that we could have life and have it more abundantly. Jesus, what a precious Gift You are! You were minding

Your own business when God Your Father asked You to give up everything to come and save us—what love.

Your **Kindness** is everlasting in Your mercy shown toward me, how can I thank You enough. I am so indebted to You.

Thank You for being a **Lifetime Partner**. After I accepted You and Your love, Your commitment to stand by me was sealed forever in heaven.

Thank You for the **Meticulous** way in which You created the earth with such variety and beauty. The timeliness of each season fills us with awe: summer's breeze, which blows ever so gently; fall's breathless colors; winter's snow, which paints a beautiful white blanket; and spring's wonderful smell of rain and flowers in bloom. The wonder of a new sunrise is as intoxicating as the view of a full moon. The ocean waves dance and stars wink at us. We behold the various flowers, the assortment of trees, and plants in all shapes and sizes. Beauty is all around us. Why? Because of the meticulous way in which You created the earth. I thank You for this and more.

You **Nursed** me back to health when I was spiritually and physically sick.

You made sure that there was no **Obstruction** between You, Your Son, and Holy Spirit as it relates to me. I don't need a third-party to reach You.

My chest swells with **Pride** when I think of how much You love me.

It's because of Your love that I don't have to **Quake** when I miss it. You have given me the authority to cleanse myself with Your Word.

Lord, Your **Reputation** has stood the test of time. It cannot be copied or surpassed.

Thank You for **S**aturating us with Your presence. There is no place we can go where You are not! What comfort!

I **T**reasure You more than anything! You **T**rust me when I can't trust myself.

Thank You for being **U**nselfish. You could have decided to let things be just You Three. But that's the kind of God You are, always thinking about me and Your creation. When we lift our hands, You only need to see our fingers to know who it is that's praising You; that's because we're **U**niquely made, and no one person's fingerprint is alike!

You could have left the earth **V**oid, but You dressed it with splendor. Thank You for choosing to have fellowship with us; it boggles the mind.

You put that **W**inning spirit on the inside of us. You **W**atch over us daily and I'm so grateful for that. **X** marks the spot in my heart reserved for You and You alone. No one or nothing can fill that spot but You.

You never **Y**ell when we make mistakes. You quietly speak to us via Holy Spirit. I'm glad You don't yell because we would probably disintegrate (smile). Thank You for taking care of me and my family and others that I love.

I would have **Z**onked out by now had it not been for You!

Each time I read this praise, I find myself adding more to it. We are all blessed beyond belief. Stop the pity party! Be grateful and give thanks!

POTPOURRI PRAISE

If ye abide in me, and my words abide in you, ye shall ask what ye will, and it shall be done unto you.

John 15:7

… in which it was impossible for God to lie…

Hebrews 6:18

As I was completing this book, I asked Holy Spirit: "What are some of the things I've forgotten to praise God for?" In His infinite wisdom, He reminded me of some things.

I began thinking about those things we tend to forget or wish to sweep under the rug. Before I continue, let me remind you that earlier I talked about being fake—not being honest. So, I must be honest and confess that I'm running out of *X, Y,* and *Z* words! If you see them omitted in any of the following praises, you add them or it's okay to not have them! You praise God because you want to, because it's right. It's not to put you in bondage because you left out a letter of the alphabet!

The next several praises represent what God gave me when I asked the question: "What did I forget that You want in this book?" I was reminded of so many things—that's why this praise is titled, "Potpourri Praise." It has a little bit of everything in it.

These next praises are so individual that I want you to pen a praise after each chapter. I know you'll be thinking of things that pertain to your life as you read them. Don't forget to read the praise first, then prop the book up and lift your hands and speak the praise from your heart again. I know the Lord will be pleased as you think and write about His goodness.

When you're ready, lift your hands and say, "Father I praise You for . . ."

My **A**uthority in the earth; my **B**usinesses; my **C**hildren and my **C**hildren's **C**hildren; I praise You for granting me some of my **D**esires.

I praise You that when I use my authority, my **E**nemies are defeated; I praise You for my church **F**amily; I thank You for my **G**uardian angels. I praise You for making me the **H**ead and not the tail. I praise You for my **I**nheritance of eternal life [Matthew 19:29 and 25:34]. I can't praise You enough for **J**esus, oh how I love that Name; Jesus, wonderful Savior, Jesus, soon and coming **K**ing.

Thank You for Your promise that says You will never **L**eave me. I praise You for being **M**aster—Ruler of all. I praise You because I'm not just a **N**umber to You, I'm special. Lord, You don't **O**ccasionally [now and then] think of me, I'm always on Your mind and I love You for it! Thank You for **P**ursuing me even when I didn't pursue You!

I **Q**uiver just thinking about Your greatness and the impact it has had on my life. I praise You for being the **R**emarkable God that You are and for making me a **S**uccess, for **T**eaching me how to love, for **U**ttering things to me by Holy Spirit that I would have otherwise never known.

I praise You for being my **V**isionary and **W**hetting my appetite for Your Word and the way You do things. I **Y**ield my tongue and praise You. The rocks will never cry out for me (Luke 19:37-40)!

I believe the Lord is pleased, but I just feel a song is what we need right now.

Go ahead, sing Him a song from your heart. Pick any song that comes to mind. If you can't think of anything, try "What a Friend We Have in Jesus" (you can Google it if you don't know it) —that one always works—or make up one yourself.

God's not picky when it comes to praise—just honored that you would honor Him.

Go ahead, write your words first.

A= _____

B= _____

C= _____

D= _____

E= _____

F= _____

G= _____

H= _____

I= _____

J= _____

K= _____

L= _____

M= _____

N= _____

O= _____

P= _____

Q= _____

R= _____

S= _____

T= _____

U= _____

V= _____

W= _____

X= _____

Y= _____

Z= _____

Now pen your praise from the words you've written:

_____

_____

_____

_____

_____

_____

_____

_____

_____

_____

_____

_____

_____

_____

_____

_____

_____

_____

_____

_____

_____

_____

Praise God For Courage

I can do all things through Christ which strengtheneth me.

Philippians 4:13

Do you know that you can do anything you put your mind to, as long as it lines up with God's Word for you?

Sure, you can. If you answered 'no' to my question, this praise will bless you. Knowing you can do something is half the battle in tackling anything. There are some things you can't do by yourself, but with Jesus you can do anything (Philippians 4:13).

What's been difficult for you? Let's tackle that thing with praise. All you need to do is add the Word of God, then listen to what Holy Spirit tells you. Remember His voice is that whisper you hear -- you may call it *your* conscience -- but most times it is Holy Spirit speaking to you. If you do what He says, the outcome will be nothing short of miraculous.

Before we begin our praise, picture that thing you wish to do but just don't have the courage to step out and do yet. Did you picture it? Did you find God's Word on it? Do you believe God is in it, and it's His desire for you to do it? Then let's praise.

Father, today I want to thank You for being my **A**nswer to this thing I didn't have the courage to attempt. You are my answer to the **B**ully who has tried to keep me bound. You're the One who turned a **C**rappy life into a Happy life. I will now **C**harge forward, because I will no longer be **D**erailed by my past and all the "can't do" thoughts. I praise You and I will no longer be **E**mbarrassed but **E**ffective, not **F**rightened but **F**earless, no longer **G**awky but **G**raceful. Thank You for **Giving** me more than I deserve. I will not be **H**indered or **H**arassed; instead, I'll **H**asten to do what You've said because my **H**elp is here—ready to make easy the task! Glory to Your Name! How can I praise You with such confidence? Because You said that I could do it, *and I will!*

You've **I**gnited a fire in me, and I thank You! I praise You for **J**olting me out of the state I was in by giving me a Holy Ghost **K**ick. Oh, it worked! Thank You, Lord. Thank You for removing **L**ayers of doubt and lifting my **M**orale. **N**o one can **N**avigate life like You, and I honor You. **O**bstacles will now be seen as **O**pportunities for You to use someone else to help me get this thing done! **P**ow! Another black eye for the devil. Oh, how I praise You! Lord, You are **Q**uite something: My **R**efuge, my **S**upport, my **T**eammate. Together we can **U**ndertake anything! I praise You that I'm no longer a **V**ictim but a **V**ictor. Thank You for **W**aking me up! Your plan has my **W**holehearted attention. I love You and I know that I'll never be the same. Thank You for **Y**anking me from my slumber so that I can reach my potential. I will no longer **Z**ig**Z**ag through life, I can be bold and just walk the straight and narrow. Thank You for helping me see that this thing will be done. I praise You for my courage. You're good, marvelous, and wonderful. Hallelujah to Your Name!

The lack of courage in your life can have devastating effects for you and those who come in contact with you. Now that you have your courage back, never give in to pressure again. Are you up to write your own courage praise? Let's do it!

Write your words first. *Carol*

A= _____

B= _____

C= _____

D= _____

E= _____

F= _____

G= _____

H= _____

I= _____

J= _____

K= _____

L= _____

M= _____

N= _____

O= _____

P= _____

Q= _____

R= _____

S= _____

T= _____

U= _____

V= _____

W= _____

X= _____

Y= _____

Z= _____

Now pen your praise from the words you've written:

_____

_____

_____

_____

_____

_____

_____

_____

_____

_____

_____

Praise God For Your Future

For I know the thoughts that I think toward you, says the Lord, thoughts of peace and not of evil, to give you a future and a hope.

Jeremiah 29:11 (NKJV)

Now that you know (or were reminded in the last Chapter) that you can do anything, and you've given God praise for the thing you thought you couldn't do, there's more. Yes, God is the energizer—He keeps going, and going, and going because there is so much to do. You have a bright future, not because I said it but because of God's Word. You may not know what the future holds but God does, so let's praise God for our future.

Father You are an **A**mazing God and I honor You this day. I can let **B**ygones be **B**ygones [forgetting the problems of the past]. Lord, for so long I tried to do things my way, but I'm going to honor You by letting You be in **C**harge of my life. You're my **C**hoice to lead and guide me. When I make **D**ecisions about my life and I factor in You, I can do more than I ever thought I could do. Father, I praise You because only You can give someone their "**D**ream job"

with no **E**xperience. I praise You for giving me Holy Spirit who is the great **E**ncourager. Thank You for helping me **F**ocus.

Goals are reachable because of You. I praise You for the opportunity of being Your child. Just knowing You Love me and knowing that You'll never give up on me has had a **H**uge impact on my life. I'm no longer **I**nsecure about the future. When I get in a **J**am, You're there to help me. Thank You, Father, I'm no longer a **K**illjoy [complainer, pessimist, worrywart], I have hope.

I praise You for taking the fear out of **L**earning. I praise You for **M**otivating me. Thank You for Your Word that **N**avigates my future. I can **O**penly discuss anything with You. I love You because it's never too late to change my **P**rofession because of You. Thank You for causing things to happen **Q**uicker than normal.

Relying on You gives me a peace no one else can give. Even when the world says I should **R**etire, You tell me to **R**e-fire into something new. I'm so **S**ecure in You. I give You praise for elevating my **T**hought life. Father, I praise You for making me **U**nique. I don't have to try to be like someone else. Doing that would only cause me to miss out on what You've called me to do. Thank You for being a **V**oice in my future. I'm no longer afraid to speak forth Your blessings God, I can speak forth the blessings of God because You have my back.

Lord, thank You for not holding against me all the **W**rong choices I've made in my life. You are the God who takes nothing and makes something out of it. I love You more with each passing day.

I get up looking ahead. **Y**ahweh, You be the Man, Lord. **Y**eah! You be the Man! And, because You are the Man, I thank You that I don't have to read **Z**odiac signs to determine my future. You've already told me what Your desire is in the Scriptures. I just need to be obedient because You've already provided a way for my success (Joshua 1:8-9). Thank You, Lord. I praise You for all that You've done!

Wow, this praise is *real*, folks, and you should be jumping for joy about your future. Be a witness to others. Let them know they don't need to call the psychic hotline! Tell them instead to call on the Lord. It amazes me when people worship the stars and ignore the One who created them!

It's praise time, write your words first.

A= _____

B= _____

C= _____

D= _____

E= _____

F= _____

G= _____

H= _____

I= _____

J= _____

K= _____

L= _____

M= _____

N= _____

O= _____

P= _____

Q= _____

R= _____

S= _____

T= _____

U= _____

V= _____

W= _____

X= _____

Y= _____

Z= _____

Now pen your praise from the words you've written:

_____

_____

_____

_____

_____

_____

_____

_____

_____

_____

_____

_____

_____

_____

_____

_____

_____

_____

_____

_____

_____

_____

_____

_____

_____

_____

_____

_____

_____

_____

_____

Don't Allow One Day
To Spoil Your Remaining Years

This is the day which the Lord has made; we will rejoice and be glad in it.

Psalms 118:24

Every day you open your eyes is a blessed day, and that's why I was compelled to write this praise. It may prove to be controversial, but I don't mean it to be. It's a praise about a horrific day in history—September 11, 2001.

Innocent people were killed, and others scarred emotionally. I'm not making light of it. It was a horrible time for our nation. I cried and prayed for our nation and those who lost loved ones along with others.

I can still tell you where I was on that day. I was at Oak Park High School in Oak Park, Michigan. I can't remember if it was for my interview or I had just started working there. We were all frozen in front of the TV in the employee lounge. Many of you, like me, can remember where you were. I didn't know of anyone who perished, but I always pray every September 11th for people who lost loved ones or close friends. But I believe that God does not want us to live the rest of our lives broken by that day and not being able to function because of the pain.

Our enemy, the devil, has kept so many people in bondage that it's difficult for them to move past that day. Sadly, what does not help, are those around us who don't want healing but want you to remain in the past and keep you with them. Why? It's a sad fact but true, some people don't want to move on. I believe it's because they don't yet know the delivering power of Jesus.

Think about this. . .Do you believe that God wants you to spend every September 11th from now on reliving the pain? If you had a loved one who perished, do you think they want you to spend every September 11th crying and distraught? I don't think so. God wants you free and they want you free as well.

I believe this is what God wants you to do. If you lost someone, get up that morning and begin to praise and thank God for the years you had with them. Thank God for the laughter and love you were able to share with them. The joyful times of fellowship. The hugs. Think about what they would want you to do on that day.

I'm speaking from experience. No, I didn't lose anyone on September 11th, but when I lost my mother, every Mother's Day was a struggle for about five years. To be honest, I don't remember how long, but it was a long time.

Even though I still had loved ones living who were mothers, like my mother-in-love, aunts, and sisters, I wouldn't even buy cards or wish them happy Mother's Day. I just pretended the day didn't exist because I didn't have my Mom.

Each Mother's Day, I'd go to the cemetery, take flowers, clean off the headstone and bawl like a baby. The worst part about this was each year I visited the cemetery, I took my three kids with me. I would encourage them to say, "Hi Grandma," not realizing the hurt and pain on their little faces.

This one particular Mother's Day while I was crying, Holy Spirit said, "Look at your kids." There they were the three of them standing, looking at me. My daughter who was around five was crying. My two sons, ages seven and twelve, were looking forlorn and helpless. Then Holy Spirit said, "Do you want to inflict your pain on them?" He then asked me, "Where do you believe your Mom is?" I answered, "With Jesus." He then said, "Do you really believe she's with Jesus?" I said, "Yes." Then He said, "Do you think she's sad?" I said, "No, I believe she's happy." He then said, "If you really believe she's with Jesus, there is no need for you to come here again and bring flowers. Instead, you should look up to heaven when you awake, smile, and tell her "Hi," and then tell her about all the times she made you laugh, how you remember her hugs and kisses. Tell her that you miss her, but you know that you'll see her again. Allow the fond memories to carry you through, and then don't come down here anymore cause she's not here!

Friends, I can't begin to tell you the freedom I felt and received that day when Holy Spirit helped me put things in perspective. That next Mother's Day, I sent out cards, called the mothers I loved, and I received the healing that I so desperately needed. There is an old saying: "Time heals all wounds." I disagree, only God can heal wounds. Only God can heal a broken heart.

While I didn't lose anyone on September 11th, I know how it feels to lose someone you love and all I can say is, once I let death go and concentrated on my mom's life with Christ, I was a better person not only for me, but for my children and all those around me.

This is why I can suggest to you that if you will get up on that day and start it with praise, the presence of Almighty God will cover you like a warm blanket in a blizzard. Your praise will set the tone for that day, and you will emerge stronger and more fulfilled as a result of your praise. You will defeat the enemy who wants to steal the day from you, and you will reign victoriously!

Determine that you are not going to allow the enemy to control you on September 11th, but you are going to make a decision on purpose to enjoy the day. No, we can't erase the past, but we can skip into the future. Let's praise.

Father, I will not feel **A**wkward today about being happy. I will not. You've been too good to me and this nation. I praise You for a **B**reakthrough this day. I call on the **C**omforter, precious Holy Spirit to move in and out of the hearts of those who lost loved ones. I will not let others **D**efine this day for me. I will praise and **E**mbrace You today. With Your help, I will keep my **E**motions in check. I will help others see Your goodness. I praise You for Your **F**aithfulness, oh **G**od, for removing **H**urts.

I will be **I**mmovable in my faith and **I**gnore the urge to follow the world. This day will not be **J**inxed but blessed. This nation will be free from any terrorist attacks. I praise You for being the **K**eeper of this nation. We will experience **L**aughter this day. Gone are the broken hearts, gone be the pain. Father, I praise You for being a **M**agnet that draws others to You by Your Love. **N**urture them as never before.

I will think of You **O**ften today. It is the only way I can be assured of success and **P**eace. I stand in the gap right now for those who are in a **Q**uandary [dilemma] today. I praise You for moving on their behalf to bring solutions right now. **R**emind them by Your Spirit that when pillows were **S**oggy with **T**ears, it was the finger of God that wiped away those **T**ears.

I honor You because our future is not **U**ncertain. We are **V**ictors, **W**arriors, there's no **Y**ellow streak down our backs. We are

Zealots [enthusiasts] for You and we choose to start this day like any other—with praise and thanksgiving!

Make sure you pray for someone else every September 11th. Take someone out to lunch or dinner that you know lost a loved one. When you see planes in the air, pray for the safety of all who are aboard. Keep the pilots and staff in prayer, especially the personnel in air traffic control. Pray that they are alert and watchful. It doesn't matter whether you know anyone who works for the airlines or someone travelling that day, they still need our prayers.

Because I'm sensitive and I know this exercise may be difficult for you, let me help you start this praise. Let's say the only **A** you can think of right now is **Anger**. Then your praise may begin something like this. . .

Jesus, Your Word says in Ephesians 4:26-27 *"Go ahead and be angry. You do well to be angry—but don't use your anger as fuel for revenge. And don't stay angry. Don't go to bed angry. Don't give the Devil that kind of foothold in your life."* (MSG) So, I'm going to do what Your Word says, while I feel angry, I'm going to praise You for letting me know through Your Word that I can let things go. I praise You for allowing me the right to feel this emotion. I'm angry at men and women who cause hurt to others, but I'm not angry at You. I'm asking that You heal not just me, but You heal angry hurt hearts all over the world.

Now proceed writing your praise from the posture of gratefulness. So, your **"B"** could say, "However, I am **B**lessed to be able to move forward and not be stuck in a negative place."

Carol

I guarantee you that if you do what I'm telling you, today will be a colossal breakthrough for you emotionally. Now you take over from here and begin to build your praise below.

A= _____

B= _____

C= _____

D= _____

E= _____

F= _____

G= _____

H= _____

I= _____

J= _____

K= _____

L= _____

M= _____

N= _____

O= _____

P= _____

Q= _____

R= _____

S= _____

T= _____

U= _____

V= _____

W= _____

X= _____

Y= _____

Z= _____

Now pen your praise from the words you've written:

_____

_____

_____

_____

_____

_____

_____

_____

_____

_____

_____

_____

_____

Praise God For
The United States Of America

> *Blessed is the nation whose God is the Lord; and the people whom he hath chosen for his own inheritance.*

Psalms 33:12

That last praise reminded me of just how blessed we are in the United States. This nation was built on godly principles, and I feel we should praise God for our nation. You may ask, "Why praise God for the United States?" Do you read the papers? Do you listen to the news and see what other countries are going through? You may say, "Have you checked out the homeless situation lately? Look how we treat these people. Look at how we do this: On and on some always see the negative."

That's precisely the kind of negative thinking you must stop. Focus instead on the good and speak blessings over our nation. No, the United States isn't perfect. You know why? I live in the United States. And if all of the millions of people were perfect but me, it still wouldn't be a perfect place, because I live here. What about you? Are you perfect? So that makes two imperfect people living in the United States. In order for something to be perfect, *everything* associated with that thing must be perfect.

We're praising God for all the wonderful things that are good about our country. And there are many wonderful things we could focus on. There's no other place I'd rather live. Sometimes I find myself singing "God Bless America." When you sing that song, believe it or not, you're speaking blessings over your nation in song; and God is pleased. If you haven't read 1 Timothy 2:1–8 recently, read it. We're admonished to pray for people in authority. Why? So we can live a quiet and peaceful life. If you're not praying, then don't complain about the state of our country. Yes, I am aware that all people are not free like those who live in the United States. That's why we need to continue to pray for other countries so they, too, will be free. We should not be satisfied until all nations are. So, join me and praise God for the United States of America (USA).

Father, thank You for blessing **America** and the **Banks** that secure our currency. I give You praise for **Corporations** that provide well-paying jobs. I praise You for such a **Developed** and productive nation. Thank You for a healthy **Economy** and the opportunity for **Education**. I praise You for **Families** who have the freedom to live in harmony with each other without being separated.

I praise You for **Governments** that protect American people at home and abroad. I praise You for the **High** standard of living we enjoy compared with other nations. I praise You for **Investment** opportunities and for **Judges** who monitor the judicial system. I praise You for **Kinsmen** who pray for this nation and support the United States as allies. I praise You for **Laws** that govern our land. I thank You that our nation is a **Melting** pot for all people.

Our **N**ation is blessed because of You! Our Nation is blessed because we recognize You! **O**pportunities are in abundance because of You. Thank You for our **P**resident who is elected by the people. I give You praise because we can own our own **P**roperty and because everything does not belong to the state. I praise You for the various **Q**uotas and how they have helped bring balance to situations that would be otherwise off balance. I give You praise for **R**estrictions on certain foods that would cause harm to our bodies.

I give You praise for **S**chools of learning for just about anything. I thank You for **T**ariffs and **T**rade, which help the economy and our system at large. I praise You for the **U**ndaunted spirit of the United States. I thank You for our ability to **V**ote. Thank You for the Veterans who have died in the past **W**ars protecting this land. I praise You that even in times of **W**ar, You provide an army to fight for our rights and the rights of others. No, Father, our nation is not perfect, but we give You praise for it anyway. We want to thank You for blessing, protecting, and providing for the United States of America. I praise You for protecting us in **Y**ears past and for future years, in Jesus' Name we give You the praise!

When you're home, sing the national anthem in your car or while you're cleaning; you're proclaiming blessings through song. I love America, and I am proud to be an American.

Write your words first.

A= _____

B= _____

C= _____

D= _____

E= _____

F= _____

G= _____

H= _____

I= _____

J= _____

K= _____

L= _____

M= _____

N= _____

O= _____

P= _____

Q= _____

R= _____

S= _____

T= _____

U= _____

V= _____

W= _____

X= _____

Y= _____

Z= _____

Now pen your praise from the words you've written:

_____
_____
_____
_____
_____
_____
_____
_____
_____
_____
_____
_____
_____
_____
_____
_____
_____
_____
_____
_____

I'm Free And I Love It!

O praise the Lord, all ye nations: praise him, all ye people.

Psalms 117:1

The Scripture above gives a mandate for nations to praise God. I know there are millions of people in the United States who praise God. I believe that's why we enjoy our freedom and wealth. After that last praise, I still have some thoughts regarding our freedom.

I don't give God praise often for freedom, so I'm just going to do it now. How about you? Let's praise.

Father, I lift my hands to You today, continuing to thank You for the freedom we enjoy. Thank You for the freedom of **A**ssembly where I can join political parties and fellowship with **B**elievers without worrying about attacks.

I thank You that freedom does not have to be **B**ought because it's free, thanks to those who fought for our freedom! Thank You, Father, for moving in the hearts of our country's forefathers to **C**ompose and put in writing the **C**onstitution. Thank You for breaking the **C**lass systems and giving freedom to all. I praise You that I live in a **D**emocratic society where equality and the

Dignity of others is largely recognized. I praise You, oh Lord, for our **E**conomic system, which is responsible in part for the wealth we have. I praise You for Holy Spirit Who acts as a **F**ilter, helping me separate good from evil and truth from lies. Thank You for the **G**overnment we have in place that is run *by* the people *for* the people. I thank You for an unselfish nation; we **H**elp other nations in recognizing the good and the bad.

I praise You for raising men and women who have fought for our **I**ndependence. I can shout the Name of **J**esus and proclaim You as Lord without any repercussions. I have access to **K**nowledge that would otherwise be hidden from me. I thank You for the due process of **L**aw in which we are innocent until proven guilty. Thank You for the **M**edia. They aren't perfect, but they do provide valuable information we need to coexist with one another. I'm not **N**aive to think my freedom came without a price; someone paid for it, and I praise You for the **M**ilitary and their obedience to fight and serve our country. I praise You for this land of **O**pportunity where I can make a difference. I thank You for freedom of the **P**ress. Though this freedom has many entities, I thank You that we can **P**ublish truths, especially the truth of Your Word. It was this freedom that gave us our Precious Bible and allowed me to write this book.

Thank You for helping me know I don't have to **Q**uake in my boots every time I see the police for fear they'll shoot me because of who I am. In the United States the police are partners. I thank You for the freedom of **R**eligion. I can practice my faith without being strong-armed by outside forces. Thank You for **S**ocial freedom whereby I can speak what I believe and go where I want to go. Thank You for our armed forces that provide protection when **T**hreats appear from our enemies. Thank You, Father, for shielding me from **U**nreasonable men and women who would take advantage of me if they could.

Thank You for giving me a **V**oice in Government. Thank You for men and women who **W**rite godly books to help us grow spiritually.

Father, I thank You for all You've done and what You'll do in the future, because You're the God who never stops giving. I'll continue to **Y**ield to You and vote as You lead. I want to keep the freedom I now enjoy. I will also remember that no matter who wins elections, Father as godly men and women pray, we can bring about a change. I know, Father, that, without Your intervention, our nation would be little more than a **Z**oo [a group marked by chaos].

People let's never take our freedom for granted. When you find yourself talking against the United States of America and your freedom, turn on the news or read the paper about how other nations are oppressed and lack the freedom we have. I'm sure this praise will be easy to write!

Write your words first.

A= _____

B= _____

C= _____

D= _____

E= _____

F= _____

G= _____

H= _____

I= _____

J= _____

K= _____

L= _____

M= _____

N= _____

O= _____

P= _____

Q= _____

R= _____

S= _____

T= _____

U= _____

V= _____

W= _____

X= _____

Y= _____

Z= _____

Now pen your praise from the words you've written:

_____

_____

_____

_____

_____

_____

_____

_____

_____

_____

_____

_____

_____

_____

_____

_____

_____

_____

_____

_____

THE EARTH BELONGS TO GOD, BUT WE GET TO ENJOY IT!

> *While the earth remaineth, seedtime and harvest, and cold and heat, and summer and winter, and day and night shall not cease.*
>
> Genesis 8:22

> *The earth is the Lord's, and the fulness thereof; the world, and they that dwell therein.*
>
> Psalms 24:1

God never lies! I'm sure that, like me, you've thought of so many things to praise God for besides what's written in this book. When we think about our nation, I remember how blessed we are to go to the store to buy food. I thought about gardens and what they produce. Isn't it amazing that the ground continues to yield from the seeds that are planted just as God promised? (Genesis 8:22) Like I said earlier. . .God never lies! If He says the ground will always produce. Guess what? The ground will always produce.

Let me now speak directly to the pessimist. Yes, I know that we have issues with pesticides and genetically modified foods. Our process is not perfect. You can find a flaw in anything if you look hard enough. But when was the last time you praised God for the very soil that yields our food? Make sure you think about this praise the next time you go to the market. Let's praise God now for the earth and the perfect way in which He made it.

Father, I praise You for the Air we breathe. I thank You for the millions of species of Animals, including those who give their lives so our bodies might be nourished. I praise You for the Beaches we enjoy, the Crops that continue to yield us food, and the various Climates we enjoy. You know it all! You made it all! I praise You for earth's perfect Distance from the sun that keeps us from burning up. Thank You for the Energy sources You supply [natural gas, coal, electricity, oil]. I praise You for the Flawless way in which You created the earth, Farmers who till the ground, Flowers that beautify, Gravitation that keeps us literally on the ground. Thank You for successful Harvests that provide for us year after year and for Your promise of everlasting and abundant life.

Thank You for metals like Iron, copper, silver, and gold that are used to make thousands of products we use daily. But I must pause here and say there is something more valuable and precious than silver and gold—a Jewel named King Jesus—oh yes!

Thank You for all things of the earth: for Lakes that provide an important source of irrigation for farmers and for fish to eat.

Thank You for the Moon that lights up the sky in the evening. I praise You for Natural resources [minerals, soils, water, forests, and fish]. I praise You for Oceans that dance. I praise You for Plant life—without it there would be no life on earth.

I praise You for the Packaging of our food, which Preserves, Protects, and keeps it fresh for distribution. I thank You for the Quality of our food partly because of the checks and balances we have in place. I praise You for Rich Soil.

I give You praise for the **S**un as it rises each morning. I praise You for the warmth and light it provides the earth. I praise You for the wonderful variety of **T**rees that give oxygen and shade. No one can **U**ndo what You've done, and I adore You. Thank You for **V**egetables that keep our bodies strong and **W**ater which is a necessity for life. Without it plants, animals, and man could not survive. Thank You because man cannot deplete the **W**ater supply; it keeps recycling itself! You are the *Original Recyclable Guru* and I give You praise.

Thank You for the **Y**ucca plants and the metallic element **Z**inc, that is so important to our steel industry.

My head swims when I think about all that You are and this is nothing compared to what You've done. What an awesome God You are! Don't tell me You don't deserve praise! I know better!

Write your words first.

A= _____

B= _____

C= _____

D= _____

E= _____

F= _____

G= _____

H= _____

I= _____

J= _____

K= _____

L= _____

M= _____

N= _____

O= _____

P= _____

Q= _____

R= _____

S= _____

T= _____

U= _____

V= _____

W= _____

X= _____

Y= _____

Z= _____

Now pen your praise from the words you've written:

_____

_____

_____

_____

_____

_____

_____

_____

_____

_____

_____

_____

_____

_____

_____

_____

_____

_____

_____

_____

_____

Praise For Inventions

I wisdom dwell with prudence, and find out knowledge of witty inventions.

Proverbs 8:12

Our Father has truly blessed us with comforts we would not want to live without. Our lives are easier because of what He's done through obedient people. When I look around my home, my hands raise with praise. What? Take a bath in a tub outside after carrying water from its source and heating it? Not necessary! I love my hot bubble baths. What about indoor plumbing in general, refrigeration, electricity, gas, and central heat and air conditioning? Even if you have only one or two of these modern inventions in your home, you have reason to praise!

This praise reflects what I see as I write. I'm sure that you're going to add your personal praise to this one, so I'm going to leave plenty of room for you to compose your praise(s). Get in the habit of praising God for everything. Get to the point where a praise is on your lips at all times. *You're going to get to the place in your life where you never complain because you're too busy praising!*

Now that you've got all the fundamentals, I want you to be free to praise using the *ABC*'s any way your imagination takes you. This is a fun praise, so bear with me while I tell you the rules. You don't have to use your *ABC's* in alphabetical order. You can even leave out some of the letters. I'm suggesting this because we must remember never to put our time with God in a box and never put God in a box. If you don't want to do all twenty-six letters of the alphabet—don't. If you want to elaborate more on one particular letter—do so. Do your own thing! You may want to do more than one praise. But remember, I'm going to have some fun praising with this one. God does laugh you know. Here we go:

Father, as I look around my home and think about where I've been, here are some things I want to praise You for. I know that You use people, but it was You who put the idea on the inside, because You were thinking about us. Therefore, I praise You for the following:

Appliances that help me with manual labor; **A**irplanes that take me from one point to the next in record time; **A**utomobiles to travel in; soft **B**eds that wrap their arms around me and make it hard for me to get up in the mornings⊠; **B**rushes and **C**ombs for my hair; **C**omputers that provide mega information; soft **C**arpet for the floors; my **C**hurch; **C**locks to tell time so I won't be late for work; beautiful **D**ishes; **F**urnaces that keep the house warm in the winter and for thermostats that allow us to switch over to cool in the summer to enjoy air conditioning; **F**ood in the **R**efrigerator; **G**arbologists who come each week and collect our waste. I praise You two times for **G**arbologists! What would we do without them!

Father, I just praise You for all **I**nventions, especially the **I**ron and **I**roning board. Thank You for **L**ights that enable me to see and a **s**witch where just a flip of the finger can turn them on or off; **M**oney to spend; **M**akeup; **O**vens to bake cakes. Thank You for **P**ens, **P**encils, and **P**aper to write with; **S**ofas to lay on to watch **T**elevision; **T**readmills to hang clothes on—I mean to exercise with ☺; **T**elevision so I can watch HGTV and *I Love Lucy* reruns; **T**oilets, thank You, Father, for inspiring someone to invent **T**oilets(!!); **V**acuums for the floors; a **W**asher and **D**ryer for my clothes; **W**indows to see Your **C**reations from; **W**indows that open to let fresh air into my home. You're just a God of too much, and I love You with all my heart!

You know what that praise reminds me of? Picture yourself as a little child with the Lord's face smiling down at you as you stand looking up at Him. You are excited for all He's provided. Then picture Him bending down so He's at your level—His face close to yours. Now, picture your little hands gently pulling His face down so you can plant a kiss on His cheek and declare, "I love You, Daddy!" That's a picture of praise. That's what God wants His children to do! Love Him! Honor Him! The Lord desires a relationship that's pure—one of respect and honor. One that's so special you can call Him Daddy. If you aren't there yet, you will be. Just keep praising, and don't forget to fight for your time with Him.

So what inventions are you thankful for? Go ahead, write your words first.

A= _____

B= _____

C= _____

D= _____

E= _____

F= _____

G= _____

H= _____

I= _____

J= _____

K= _____

L= _____

M= _____

N= _____

O= _____

P= _____

Q= _____

R= _____

S= _____

T= _____

U= _____

V= _____

W= _____

X= _____

Y= _____

Z= _____

Now pen your praise from the words you've written:

_____

_____

_____

_____

_____

_____

_____

_____

_____

_____

_____

_____

_____

_____

_____

_____

_____

_____

_____

_____

_____

_____

When The Enemy Goes Low--You Go High!

From the mouths of children and babies come songs of praise to you. They sing of your power to silence your enemies who were seeking revenge.

Psalms 8:2-3 (ESV)

It's hard to say good-bye when penning a book like this. How do you end a book of Praise? I don't know how. When I think I'm done, more praises come. Psalms 34:1 says, *"I will bless the Lord at all times: his praise shall continually be in my mouth."* So, because praise should be continuous, I guess I'll be adding to this book forever!

At the 2016 Democratic National Convention, Michelle Obama first uttered her now-famous catchphrase: "When They Go Low, We Go High" while discussing how to "handle bullies" in support of Hillary Clinton's bid for the White House. Her motto quickly caught on.

Well, we have a spiritual enemy, a bully: his name is Satan. When the enemy goes low, trying to tell you what you can't do, and that God has forsaken you -- go high!! Remind your enemy through your praise that God is for you, not against you.

We are in a spiritual war. Your enemy is always speaking deceptive lies. He wants to tell us who we aren't and who we are. But we must be persistent in telling him who we really are according to God's Word. So, I've appropriately named this praise, "When the Enemy Goes Low. . .You Go High!" You do that by confessing who God says you are and giving God praise. That's how you shut your enemy's mouth and any other voice that tries to discourage you.

The difference in this praise and those in this book is that you'll pen most of it yourself. I'll give you a few examples, but I don't know what negative voices are telling you. I say voices because your enemy (Satan) isn't the only one who will say negative things to you. It could be a co-worker, a friend and in some sad cases, it could be your mom, dad, or a sibling. AND -- the worse voice is your own voice. You'll believe you, so you need to watch what you are saying to yourself. If the voices are not saying what God says about you, don't receive it -- I don't care who it is!

Satan's tactics never change. He uses the same five tools found in Mark 4:17-19 which are, Affliction (trouble), Persecution (people), the Cares of this World (sickness i.e., Covid, cancer, migraines, etc.), the Deceitfulness of Riches (fooled by money or the lack thereof), and the lusts (anything you feel you have to have, but you don't have it, so you chase after it) among other things - to try and keep the Word from becoming deeply planted in your life. Don't buy the lie!!!

Here are some examples of what I mean. . .

When the enemy tells you that you'll never **Amount** to anything . . .you tell him that your future is bright and praise God, He said, **"Before** I formed you in your mother's womb God set you apart for victory" (Gloria Pruett paraphrase of Jeremiah 1:5). Tell the negative voices that in Jeremiah 29:11 God went on to say. . . "For I know the thoughts that I think toward you, saith the Lord, thoughts of peace, and not of evil, to give you an expected end." Tell the negative voices, "I know my end and it's good -- how about yours!!!"

If the accuser says you're a **Failure** because you've Failed so many times, you'll never get it right. You begin to praise God with the Scripture that says, "Though a righteous man fall seven times, he'll still rise every time." (Proverbs 24:16)

When the enemy tells you that you are **Helpless,** remind Him of who your **Helper** is. Lift up your eyes to the hills from where our help comes from (Psalms 121:1-2). Point to yourself and remind yourself that Holy Spirit our Helper lives in us, and He will never leave us! John 16:7 says it like this in the New King James Version, "Nevertheless I tell you the truth. It is to your advantage that I go away; for if I do not go away, the Helper will not come to you; but if I depart, I will send Him to you." Never buy the helpless lie again!

When the enemy tells you, "**Everyone** is against you. No one **Likes** you. You don't have any friends, you go high by saying, "If God be for me, and He is, it doesn't matter if the world is against me! I have the best Three Friends ever who will never leave me. God my Father, Jesus my Savior and Lord, and Holy Spirit my Friend and Comforter. I'm good!!" (Romans 8:31)

Voices will tell you that you're **Stupid.** You go high by saying, "You obviously don't know how **Smart** I really am. I guess you don't know Genesis 1:26-27. Let me tell you what it says. . .26 And God said, Let us make man in our image, after our likeness: and let them have dominion over the fish of the sea, and over the fowl of the air, and over the cattle, and over all the earth, and over every creeping thing that creepeth upon the earth. 27 So God created man in his own image, in the image of God created he him; male and female created he them. "I'm far from **Stupid**, I have wisdom and words I haven't even used yet!!"

Voices say, "God won't help you out of this mess. You're in **Trouble** now!" You say, "I am not forsaken. . .God is in me and for me. His Word says in Hebrews 13:5 that He will never leave me, nor forsake me."

Don't let negative voices pull you down. . .when voices go low. . .you go high!! Come on, declare some things. . .pen your praise. . ."*When they go low, we go high!*"

Write your words based on what I've shared in the paragraphs above. It will look something like this. Say what the negative voices are saying then you counter.

A= You'll never Amount to anything! Not so! _____

B= _____

C= _____

D= _____

E= _____

F= I'm a Failure -- Nope I Get Up _____

G= _____

H= You are Helpless -- NO, I'm not, I have a Helper _____

I= _____

J= _____

K= _____

L= No one Likes you -- "Really, last I checked God gave His Son Jesus for me! And Jesus is my Friend." Then Jesus turned around and gave me another Friend, Holy Spirit. I'd say, "I'm Liked by those who matter. Who Likes you?"_____

M= _____

N= _____

O= _____

P= _____

Q= _____

R= _____

S= The enemy says you're Stupid. You say, "Go read Genesis 1:26-27. Cause ain't nobody got time for you!" _____

T= You're in Trouble. "No, I'm not! God is with me, and there is nothing He can't handle!" _____

U= _____

V= _____

W= _____

X= _____

Y= _____

Z= _____

Now pen your praise from the words you've written:

_____

_____

_____

_____

_____

_____

_____

_____

_____

_____

_____

_____

_____

_____

_____

_____

_____

_____

A LETTER OF RECOMMENDATION

While I live will I praise the Lord: I will sing praises unto
my God while I have any being.

Psalms 146:2

Earlier, we talked about how important it is to know God before
you can praise appropriately. As I gave this more thought, I did
not want to end this book without somehow portraying my love
and respect for a Man who has blessed me beyond measure. His
credentials stand alone; however, the thought ran across my mind
that there may be some of you who still don't really know who this
Man is. So, I thought I would write a "letter of recommendation"
for the Person I'm asking you to get to know. Please understand
that this letter of recommendation is not based on what I've
heard—but experienced:

August 18, 2004

To Those Who May Not Know:

It is my sincere desire that you get to know God and His Son Jesus
with your heart and not your head. You see, the One I affectionately
*call Daddy is **A**vailable to His kids twenty-four-seven, three hundred*
*and sixty-five days a year. He **B**alances His time well and His **B**enefits*
are off the chart.

His Character is impeccable; His Decision-making skills are the best of the best. He brings Energy to the relationship every day. Your visits never bore Him.

He's Fair in the judgment of others. He provides unlimited Growth to all who call Him Lord. He judges the Heart and not your education, income or social status. He saw to it that you'd have a BFF (Best Friend Forever) in the earth. His Name is Holy Spirit.

People all over the world covet His Interpersonal skills and want to be just like Him. You never have to Jostle with others for His time or His blessings; He has more than enough for everyone. There is no one on the face of the earth who does not Know of Him. However, Knowing Him on a personal level should be your priority.

This Man is in a League all by Himself. His Management style cannot be duplicated because He makes no Mistakes and does not Neglect His duties. Oblivious to your feelings—never. He does not need a Planner for appointments or Personal data. He knew you before you were born. Even though He's the Boss who owns everything, He'll be Quiet and allow you to Reject His best-laid plans for your life.

He won't give up on you. Once you get on target and realize what you've missed, He will Restore those things, and He's never said to me once, "I told you so!" His Retirement plan cannot be duplicated.

His deals are Sealed with the Blood of His Son, not a pen. He will Train you until you get it right, and He performs all of His exit interviews. You always have His Undivided attention. You don't need anyone to Validate your credentials. He gave you every credential you need. He told you that you can do all things through His Son Jesus Christ which strengthens you.

Workers' compensation is not an option, because this Person you're building a relationship with sent His Son to earth to die so you could live. You can bring all your aches, pains, and scars to Him because

*His Son paid the price for all aches and pains on the cross. He's the Healer. Although He's in love with billions of people, when you talk to Him, it's as if you were the only person in the **W**orld.*

*We were nothing, but He proves mathematics to be in the wrong, because our nothing **X** [times] His something = everything. Time spent with Him is **Y**ummy. Being accepted as His daughter was the **Z**enith in my life.*

I've given you a heads up. The decision is yours. He has everything to offer, and you have everything to gain. Don't be unwise; accept His love and eternal life by accepting His Son Jesus Christ as Lord and Savior. You'll be sorry if you don't.

Sincerely,
Gloria P. Pruett,
The King's Daughter

THIS CHAPTER IS EXTRA SPECIAL!

Why art thou cast down, O my soul? And why art thou disquieted in me? Hope thou in God: for I shall yet praise him for the help of his Countenance.

Psalms 42:5

People talk about being in the presence of "movers and shakers." If you have received Jesus as your Lord and Savior, you join me in having the ultimate Movers and Shakers on our side: God the Father, God the Son, and God Holy Spirit. It can't get *any* better than that! They know how to get any job done.

Our Savior, Jesus, is always there to help us. He petitions the Father on our behalf. Do you know Him as Savior? Is He Lord of your life? If not, He can become your Lord by confessing the following prayer. It is that simple. Don't try to complicate it. The only prerequisite to saying this prayer is that you must mean what you say with your heart. The world will try to tell you that it's more complicated than it is, but trust me, it isn't.

The prayer is based on Romans 10:8–10, which says: *"But what saith it? The word is nigh thee, even in thy mouth, and in thy heart: that is the word of faith, which we preach; That if thou shalt confess with thy mouth the Lord Jesus, and shalt believe in thine heart that*

God hath raised him from the dead, thou shalt be saved. For with the heart man believeth unto righteousness; and with the mouth confession is made unto salvation. "

If you're sincere about making Jesus Lord over your life, repeat this prayer by saying it out loud so that you can hear yourself. Mean it in your heart, and you will be saved right where you are. As I said earlier, don't try to make this complicated, just receive. If you're ready to receive Jesus, just say this prayer out loud right where you are. . .

> Dear Lord Jesus, I believe that You are the Son of God. I believe that You died on the cross at Calvary, bearing all of my sins for me. They put You in a grave, but I believe that You are no longer there. I believe that You rose from the dead and that You are alive right now. Thank You, Lord, for hearing my prayer. Thank You, Lord, for answering my prayer and coming into my life right now. I believe with my heart, and I confess with my mouth that Jesus is now my Lord, Savior, and Master, and as of right now, according to Your Word, "I am born again!"

If you just prayed that prayer, you are now "born again" and your name has been written in the Lamb's Book of Life (Revelation 21:27). When you pass from this world, you will be heaven bound.

Some time ago, Holy Spirit gave me a poem for people just like you who prayed this prayer. He wanted you to know how God feels about you now that you've accepted Jesus—His Son—as

Lord. Please allow this poem to minister to you as it did me when Holy Spirit gave it to me.

I've been waiting for this day with anticipation you see,
When in your heart you would decide to believe in Me.
Your name is now written in the Lamb's Book of Life.
One day we will be united like a husband and wife.
A home in eternity that's where you'll live—
It will be your new "hood."
You only get there by accepting Me—not by being "good."
But remember that salvation is just a start.
To develop an intimate relationship would be smart.
Please get to know Holy Spirit, your Earthly Friend--
Who'll lead and guide you right until the end.
Yes, all the angels in heaven are rejoicing you see,
At the decision you made to confess and accept Me!

Authored by Gloria P. Pruett

Closing Words

He who brings an offering of praise and thanksgiving honors and glorifies Me: and he who orders his way aright [who prepares the way that I may show him], to him I will demonstrate the salvation of God.

Psalms 50:23 (AMP)

I have been blessed to share with you some of the secrets I use when praising the Lord. As you take your praise to a higher level, take others with you—share the experience of praise.

If you're not attending a church—find one. You need to be around other believers so you can grow and be strengthened (Hebrews 10:25). Please know that they are people first, so don't look for perfection. Get into a good Bible teaching church so you can grow in God.

You Pen The End

Bless the Lord, O my soul. O Lord my God, thou art very great; thou art clothed with honor and majesty.

Psalms 104:1

The final pages are reserved for you—yes, you! I want you to write your own ending to this book. I want you to do what I've taught you. Begin to pen words to the Lord. Then, write your praise from the words. Always refer to previous pages and continue to add on using as many notebooks as you can fill.

Peace to you my brothers and sisters. Know that if I never meet or see you in this life, if you've confessed Jesus as your Lord and Savior, we will meet one day. Until then, keep the pen to the paper. The Lord is waiting—**GO**, write some praises!

—Gloria P. Pruett!

Alphabets I Didn't Use In A Praise

When I wrote this book in 2005, I promised God that I would not stop praising Him. You see, praise for me is an expression of my love and appreciation for all that God has done for me and He's done a lot. And because He never stops blessing, I'll never stop praising.

I also told God I would not write a book and then have others praise Him while I stopped. No, He's too Good for that!! So, the praises listed here were not used in the book as a Chapter lesson, but they are what I continued to write.

What you are about to read are handwritten praises that I wrote in the white spaces of my personal praise book. Even though they were written at random, I put them in alphabetical order here. Please know I'll continue to write praises to God until I no longer have breath in my body!! I'm just honored that God gave me a second chance to re-birth this book. You will note that not all alphabets are represented. I just write and praise, write and praise. But that's where you come in, You add to this book and, before you know it, pages will be filled with praises you've penned on your own.

A

God, I praise you because there is not **Anybody, Anywhere** who cares for and loves me like You do.

Jesus, my **Ability** to do anything is enlarged because I involve You and Holy Spirit.

Jesus, Thank You for being an **Active** God – One who moves on my behalf.

God You are the **Antidote** for any venom the devil tries to send my way.

Jesus, thank You for being the **Artist** who paints my picture of life in colors and scenery no man can duplicate. Your supernatural paint brush has and is still creating awesome pictures beyond my wildest dreams.

Jesus, I thank You for Your **Ability** on me to do and be **Anything** You've created me to be.

B

Thank You for helping me get out of the **Boat** of timidity and enabling me to walk on the water of life!

C

Thank You Holy Spirit for being my Spiritual **Caffeine**, my stimulant, that increases the activity in my brain and nervous system with no negative side effects.

God I'm so grateful that your **Calendar** is never too full for me. You've never told me to "Talk to the Hand." I've been blessed to have Face-to-Face communication with you always.

Jesus, thank you for being my **Covering**.

Thank You Three, God My Father, Jesus my Lord and Savior, and Holy Spirit my Friend for never giving me the **Cold Shoulder**.

Heavenly Father, thank You for the dispensation of grace and for being a **Compassionate** God!

Jesus I'm **Content** in you – happy, satisfied and delighted.

Holy Spirit, thank You for **Checking** me when I get off track. You never **Condemn** me; You only **Correct** me, which helps me get right back on track. Thank You for Your **Constant Care**.

Jesus, thank you for letting me **Crawl** into your arms to receive **Comfort**.

Father, You've made it so **Convenient** for me to love You. Thank You for the Simplicity of our relationship.

Jesus, You are my **Champion**. You conquered death and hell for me and took the keys of death and hell from our enemy. (Revelation 1:18) And just like a real Champion, there is no locksmith living that can duplicate those keys and return them to the devil. (Holy Spirit gave this to me one night while studying, and it blesses me every time I praise God with this one).

D

I praise You for being a **D**ependable God!

Jesus, thank You for being my **Defender**, You've given me Angels that protect me and those I love day and night.

Jesus, I praise You for not putting **Distance** between us.

God, my **Dependence** for provision is on You alone and I'm so thankful that I have You.

Holy Spirit, thank You for helping me to be **Disciplined**. It's life changing, and I'm thankful for the person I'm becoming with Your help.

E

Jesus, You are the Chief **Economist** in my life. You track my seeds sown and finances so that I have more than enough wealth to be a blessing in the earth with money left over for myself!

Jesus, You are the Master **Encourager**! After all it was You who told me in Philippians 4:13 that "I can do all things through Christ (that's you) which strengtheneth me."

Holy Spirit, You are my **Energizer** when I have no strength. You power me up with Your words of **Encouragement**, and I find myself **Energized** for any task at hand.

Jesus, I praise you that when the **Earthquakes** of life came, You were and will always be there to steady my feet. Because of You I found myself still standing when others around me crumbled.

I'm **Eager** to praise You Three, God my Father, Jesus my Lord and Holy Spirit my Helper, because there is so much for which to praise You.

Jesus, thank You for **Embracing** me with love and tenderness.

God, You are **Extremely** good to me and my family. You protect us, You watch over us, You provide peace, comfort and so much more, and I'm truly grateful!

F

Jesus, thank you for being **Faithful**. When I look at my life, I see your **Fingerprint** of **Faithfulness.** Everywhere I look and as far as my eyes can see, Your **Faithfulness** is before me!

Thank You Holy Spirit for allowing me to **Frolic** in my praise – let my hair down, kick up my heels – it's so much **Fun** to dance and sing in Your presence. Thank You for the new songs You provide that enhance my praise to God.

Jesus, Your Word has changed my **Focus** in life, my **Focus** is on You and my life is the better because of it.

Jesus, I'm so appreciative that You've conquered every **Foe** in my life: the **Foe** of lack, the **Foe** of fear, the **Foe** of depression, the **Foe** of sickness and disease. If it has a name, You've conquered it, and I'm grateful to You.

Thank you for taking the **Fragments** of my life and putting them back together again. Unlike Humpty Dumpty, I don't depend on king's men or king's horses to put me back together. When I fall; my dependance is on the King of kings, Jesus --You're that Name! Too bad poor Humpty Dumpty didn't know You!

G

Lord, thank You for the Supernatural **Growth** I've experienced in my life because of Your Word and Your Spirit in Me. I don't even recognize myself when I think back over the years. I am truly grateful! And I praise You in advance for the **Growth** I'll continue to experience as I stay close to and obey Your Word and the voice of Holy Spirit!

Lord, You are the **Glue** that keeps me together when the world tries to pull me apart. Their attempts won't work.

Thank You Jesus for not holding **Grudges**. Thank you for **Giving** me more than I deserve.

Jesus, I celebrate Your victory over the **Grave** and I thank You for that same Power living in me.

Thank You for being a **Global God** – there is no place I can go where You are not.

Thank you for **Guiding** me even when I was blinded by the world's system. You **Guided** me to victory, and I'm so thankful.

H

Heavenly Father, I'm **Honored** that You would accept me as Your daughter.

Holy Spirit, You're the **Hug** I long for each day. Waking up knowing that You're with me is the comfort I so need. I guess that's one of the reasons Jesus gave You to me -- I feel safe knowing that You are with me.

Jesus, thank You for not leaving the care of Your children to a **Hired Hand,** because John 10:12 NLT tells us that a **Hired Hand** will run when the enemy comes, but You are our Shepherd that yields a rod and staff. You beat off anything that comes to kill, steal, and destroy. You watch over us, and I am so Grateful!

I

Jesus, thank you for giving me the best **Instructor** in life – Holy Spirit.

Thank You Lord for never **Ignoring** my cries for help!

Holy Spirit, thank you for the **Intimacy** I share with You -- just us two. You make me feel special.

J

Holy Spirit, thank you for helping me to not be **Judgmental.**

Jesus, I'm so grateful that I don't have to **Jump** through hoops or people for You to hear me; my petitions are heard the moment they're spoken – Thank You!

K

Jesus, thank You for increasing my **Knowledge** about You, My Heavenly Father, and Holy Spirit through Your Word.

L

Jesus, You are my **Light** in the darkness. Thank You for Your light that allows me to see where I need to go.

M

Holy Spirit my Guide, thank You for helping me **Maneuver** through the land mines of life. If not for You, I would have blown up spiritually.

Father, Son, and Holy Ghost, You are truly what **Matters Most**.

My **Memory** is blessed because of Holy Spirit. Thank You for helping me recall everything.

O

Jesus, it's comforting to know that Your Word will never become **Obsolete!** Thank You for Your Word that keeps me grounded.

Holy Spirit, thank You for helping me stay away from **Offense**. I can remain peaceful because of You! You calm me down. You're the greatest Helper ever!

Thank You Jesus for the many **Opportunities** You've provided through the doors You've opened.

P

Holy Spirit my Friend, I thank You that **Pleas** for wisdom are always heard and You always come through.

Holy Spirit, thank you for your **Personal Participation** in my life. You don't send a representative. You're here for me 24/7/365 and I'm honored to have You as my Friend living in me.

Father God, thank You for being such a **Passionate** God. You're so loving and **Passionate** about me. After all, You had Your Son die for me. You've provided healing for me. You've provided safety for me. You've given me a sound mind full of power, too many benefits to name that You've bestowed upon me. If that isn't **Passionate**, what is!

Q

Jesus, I never **Question** Your love. You've made it quite clear that nothing I could ever do will separate me from Your love (Romans 8:38-39).

Thank You Jesus for providing **Quiet** moments for me to think.

Jesus, I never have to **Quail** (cower, to recoil in dread; to make fearful) in Your presence. Your love for me quiets my spirit and allows me to come boldly to You so I can listen and learn.

R

Jesus, it's comforting to know that I'm always on Your **Radar**. Who else would sit and intercede for me day and night at the right hand of the Father pleading my case daily? No one would do that for me but You, and I'm thankful.

Thank You for the **Restart** Button I have when I sin, found in I John 1:9. When I push that button and confess my sin, Your Word says You forgive me, and I'm confident in Your Word. You never lie, and Your Word declares that forgiveness is mine the minute I come to You acknowledging my sin and asking for forgiveness. Thank you for your faithfulness to forgive me every time. Your endless forgiveness is a treasured gift.

S

Holy Spirit, thank You for not just being a **Spectator** in my life, but You are an active Participant, and I love it!

Jesus, I'm not **Scared** of the future because He who holds the future, also holds my hand. You're with me, and You promised that You would never leave me. So, I'm not **Scared** anymore!

Jesus, because of You, I can remain **Sane** in this world in which I live. Your Word tells us what would happen in the last days, but You said, fear not because You're with me, so I choose to "Fear Not,…" (Isaiah 41:10)

Father, You're such a **Special** God – Everything You do is above amazing.

Lord, thank You for Your **Strength** that You give. When I feel like I can't go on, it is Your **Strength** that sustains me!

Holy Spirit, thank You as my Helper for pulling Holy Ghost **Strings,** using Your influence and favor with powerful people, to make things happen in my life that I couldn't make happen.

Jesus, I thank you for the **Security** You provide. I don't need iron bars or steel doors to keep the enemy out. You've given me angels to encamp about me, and they work!!

Jesus, I thank You for revealing Yourself to me. You are not a **Statue** that I pray to, You're a Living God, risen Savior, My Friend and Helper.

T

Lord Jesus, I praise You for being the greatest **Treasure** I've ever found!

Holy Spirit, Thank You for **Taming** the voices in my head when my mind wants to go **Tilt.** I'm no longer afraid of the **Threats** from the enemy. You are well prepared to help me and deliver me from **Toxic** thoughts!

Heavenly Father, when **Trials** and **Troubles** come, and **Times** are **Tough,** I'll remember whose child I am – that I belong to You and You can handle anything!

Thank You for causing me to **Triumph** in life when failure seems eminent.

U

Jesus, You are **Unlike** anything ever!!! Whatever I need, You're it! When my focus is on You, I am **Unafraid** to tackle the issues of life.

Jesus, I thank You for the **Unshakeable** faith and confidence that I have in You as my Savior.

Holy Spirit, thank You for Your **Undivided** attention You give me. When I talk to You, You are only concerned with me! And, You never leave me no matter how crazy I act. Jesus gave You to me, and You're here with me for the long haul. Thank You.

Heavenly Father, I have no **Uncertainty** when it comes to my future – it's bright because of the promises in Your Word that You spoke over me as Your child.

V

Lord Jesus, thank you for being my **Vindicator**! I don't have to plan revenge, because Your Word declares that **Vengeance** belongs to You. When someone messes with me, I have the assurance that You got this! (Romans 12:19)

If I so choose, and I should, I can approach each day with **Vigor** (be active, have mental strength) because of the Greater One in me, none other than Holy Spirit.

Jesus, thank You for making me a **Victor** and not a Victim!

W

Jesus, thank You Lord for helping me **Weather** the storms in my life.

Jesus, I praise You for Your **Willingness** to love me despite my shortcomings.

Holy Spirit, thank You for Your **Wisdom**, You make me **Wiser**!

Jesus, thank You for Your **Watchful** eye over my life and those I love and hold dear. I can remain calm, because You never slumber nor sleep. Thank You for **Watching** over me, my family and those I love. (Psalms 121:4)

Heavenly Father, when I look at each day You've made and the beauty in it, all I can say is You are a **WOW** God!

Holy Spirit, thank You for Your Counsel, because of it, I can **Wisk** away (brush off) disappointments, because You provide the Godly perspective I need to keep going!

Z

Jesus, I praise You because when I feel low, I can look forward to a positive **Zap** (a sudden forceful positive blow) in my finances, in my relationships, in my spiritual growth, really in every area of my life. So, I praise You, in advance, for providing that **Zap**!

Well, this is it for me right now. I've provided some blank pages for you to continue to write this book to make it your own. I know God our Father, Jesus our Savior, and Holy Spirit our Friend will be pleased with whatever you write and praise. Remember, for these last pages, just pen praises, don't try to put them in alphabetical order, just find new ways to praise!

Empty Page to Pen Your Praise!

_____

_____

_____

_____

_____

_____

_____

_____

_____

_____

_____

_____

_____

_____

_____

_____

_____

_____

_____

_____

_____

Empty Page to Pen Your Praise!

_____

_____

_____

_____

_____

_____

_____

_____

_____

_____

_____

_____

_____

_____

_____

_____

_____

_____

_____

_____

_____

_____

Empty Page to Pen Your Praise!

Empty Page to Pen Your Praise!

_____

_____

_____

_____

_____

_____

_____

_____

_____

_____

_____

_____

_____

_____

_____

_____

_____

_____

_____

_____

_____

_____

_____

Empty Page to Pen Your Praise!

CPSIA information can be obtained
at www.ICGtesting.com
Printed in the USA
LVHW080325241222
735796LV00030B/648